the

Woman

from the

Wisemore

Doris Stanton's Story

Copyright © 2019 Dawn Parton

Published by PPR Publishing,
19 Kingswell Road, Northampton NN2 6QB

www.pprpublishing.co.uk

A CIP catalogue record for this book
is available from the British Library.

ISBN: 978 1 9164347 2 1

Printed and bound in Great Britain by IngramSpark /
Lightning Source UK Ltd.

Acknowledgements

There are some wonderful people whose kindness and support helped Mom, and also helped the family through the worst time when Mom passed. I know she would want me to thank them all on her behalf.

To the staff at St Giles in Lichfield, who supported Mom when she first came out of hospital.

To the staff at Stoke Hospital for getting her through pneumonia and for helping with special wedding arrangements, so Mom could see Charlie and Samantha get married.

To the Stoke Registrar and Cannock Registrar for liaising to make the wedding possible for Mom to see.

To the Honey Rose Foundation for making Mom's wish come true, to see her grandson married.

To the social workers from Staffordshire Social Services who visited Mom and who showed her nothing but kindness and compassion.

To Mickey, for coming to see Mom before her passing, and for the support he has given me.

To John, for bringing the honey for Mom to take, even though at first she hated it! She did eventually grow to like it.

To Mo, for giving Mom a real purpose, knitting tiny clothes for the premature babies in hospital, and to Sarah, for letting her knit jumpers for the girls, who Mom always commented were beautiful and so well mannered.

To all the staff from Colliery Practice, for both surgery appointments and home visits, with extra special thanks to the nurse who was with Mom when she passed.

To the George Stacey Funeral Home in Hednesford, for their care and compassion while remaining truly professional throughout.

To The Church of Our Lady of Lourdes in Hednesford, for the beautiful funeral service and their continued support.

To Staffordshire police, for their support and for providing specialist victim support. Police work these days covers much more than the uniform suggests.

An extra big thank you goes to Maggie Allen, for her compassionate approach to writing Mom's book. When Mom first met Maggie, she knew there was no-one better who she could trust to do justice to her life story. She was drawn to Maggie because of the writer's true empathy for the life Mom had lived. I know Mom would be very happy with the finished book.

Thank you, everyone.
Dawn Parton

"Never forget where you come from."

Doris Stanton (8.3.1930 – 26.1.2018)

Foreword

You don't have to be highly educated to have wisdom. My mother was proof of that. My mother, Doris Stanton, had the wisdom of a wickedly hard life.

I spoke to her when I was thinking of writing my book (*Breaking the Chain*, 2014) because I wanted to tell my story, not to gain people's sympathy or praise, but in the hope that my own experiences could help others whose lives had taken a really bad turn.

My message was that, no matter how bad your life may be right now, you can still change it.

I needed to know that Mom would be comfortable with my story being told, out there for the whole world to see. And she was. She was proud of me and she supported me in my decision – even though my story would tell of a dysfunctional family life with many bad aspects, and she was the mother in that family.

Reading my book led her to think about writing her own life story, and when she eventually came to live with me and my family after Dad died, she began opening up to me about her past – her childhood, her losses, her pain and her struggles, the fights and the

1

friendships – everything I'd never known about her. But always about her determination and her survival.

These chats we had, when it was just the two of us with a cup of tea and a biscuit, started to build a bridge between us, a bridge that spanned the distance created by those things in our family past that had – beyond our control – caused secrecy and lies, fear and damage, so much damage. With this bridge, our mother-daughter relationship blossomed and we were able to discuss those things that had been taboo – the abuse we had both suffered at the hands of those who were supposed to love and care for us.

This was another part of a total healing process.

When she was diagnosed with cancer and I was faced with losing my best friend, I don't think I would have got through that time in one piece without the help and support of my brother, Nigel, and sister, Brenda. When Mom did slip away, my brother, Shaun, and his partner, Wayne, helped tremendously with choosing her special final outfit and some beautiful flowers.

Many people avoid talking about death, especially their own, and that's perfectly understandable. But I know now that if we put aside our fear of the subject and speak to those closest about how we would like our death to be recognised and our life celebrated, even discussing details of the funeral and what kind of send-off we'd like, this makes it so much easier for those left behind because, after we are gone, they can have peace of mind in the knowledge that they carried out our final wishes and gave us the ending we wanted.

So, my message to everyone is, please don't be afraid to talk about death. We all have to meet it one day, and surely it must be better to do so, knowing every detail of our special plans has been discussed, agreed and arranged.

Peace of mind, for everyone.

It's such a pity that Mom passed away before she'd finished telling me the whole story, but she was ready to go, it was her time. Hers is still a great story – a story of a wonderful woman. ***The Woman from the Wisemore***

Dawn Parton

FROM THE BEGINNING

Walsall,1930. The dingy, dilapidated rows of blackened terraced houses in The Wisemore, a raggy-arsed area close to the railway where the stench of poverty mingled with steam-engine smoke and chimney soot on a daily basis and clung to the buildings, to the people, to the very fabric of their existence.

On the eighth day of the month of March that year, as Spring was emerging from the winter smog, I made my own entrance into this coal-blackened world, my bawling objections to the bleak surroundings echoing around the faded wallpaper and rattling windows of Number Five, School Street.

"It's a girl!"

"It's another mouth to feed, that's what it is."

The exhausted, sweat-drenched mother sighed the sigh of a woman moulded by hard graft and life-long worry, who'd just pushed and yelled her way through childbirth. "Well, now we got a girl, there won't be no more."

I had two older brothers, Richard, the eldest – known as Dickie – and Alan. There would have been a third boy but James, someone I was fated never to know, had died in his childhood before I had the chance. No matter how hard life makes you, it's that kind of thing that never goes away, never stops hurting. No matter how you hide the pain.

Our family. My mom, Alice, and my dad, Alf. Mr and Mrs Alfred Bough, the boys, and now me, too. They named me Doris.

Dad, he worked down the pit. Littleton Colliery in Huntington, on the outskirts of Cannock Chase.

> The history of coal mining in Huntington goes back hundreds of years, but Littleton Pit had a very unfortunate start when the first shaft was sunk in 1877 by the Cannock & Huntington Colliery Company. They were only down to a depth of 438 feet when water burst in and flooded the shaft, resulting in the mining company being wound up in 1884.
>
> Later, in 1897, Lord Hatherton, a wealthy landowner, commissioned the sinking of a second shaft, and by February 1899 this one had reached a depth of 1644 feet. There was an attempt to recover the first shaft but that was eventually abandoned.
>
> This pit became one of the largest coalmines in the Midlands and it was one of the last collieries to remain on Cannock Chase.

Terraced houses joined in a single row, weary old

sentries of brick and mortar along the winding Stafford Road, chimney stacks puffing like the pipes of the old men in the pub, and the pit head winding gear standing tall into the sky, looming over the rooftops. A chain of empty rail trucks shunting in, shiny black coal tumbling down the chutes until every truck was piled high, then the chain would chug on its way, with the familiar rhythm of metal wheels on the railway track.

Mom had a job in the Bullows Long Street Works in Walsall.

Alfred Bullows & Sons Ltd, established in 1835 and originally a manufacturer of metal buckles, later expanding into general ironmongery and from there into air compressors and paint sprayers. Like many companies in metalwork and engineering, Bullows would soon become the munitions factory, producing hand grenades. The AB&S Mills 36M grenade.

That's what my mom did.

The third of September, 1939. The deep voice of a man, calm and well spoken, came from the radio to tell the people we were at war with Germany. I was nine.

My brothers and I would go visit Nan and Pop Brough once a fortnight. I remember one time the boys were jumping back and forth between the boats on the canal and I thought it looked like great fun, so I joined in. I was wearing my nice new pleated dress and should have known it was a bad idea, but I jumped anyway. Next thing I knew, I was in the water and my dress was

7

filthy and soaking wet. Dickie and Alan had to haul me out and when we got back to the house, Nan wailed my legs for what I'd done. It was the first time I'd ever been smacked.

In the 1700s the rapid growth of the mining industries in the Birmingham area created a demand for a means of transport to move the heavy loads of coal and limestone from the Black Country to the factories and manufacturing plants where they were needed. This type of haulage would not be able to rely on the roads in the area, many of which were subject to being damaged following periods of heavy rain, with some routes becoming quite dangerous to use.

An Act of Parliament, passed on the twenty-fourth of June 1783, enabled the local canal system to be developed, and the Toll End branch of the Birmingham canal, extending the line from Broadwaters, opened to Walsall in June 1799.

Canal carrying companies sprang up, and the numbers of horse-drawn boats increased to meet the need to move the heavy cargos, and soon the canal boat business enjoyed great wealth.

Large factories were built along the route of the canal, offering increased employment opportunities and in turn expanding the population of local towns as people moved into the area to find work.

Prosperity lifted the spirits of the people, with

improved transport, large-scale manufacturing, lower prices on consumer goods, and a much wider choice of stock in the shops.

The canal network later linked through to some sea ports, enabling the export of manufactured goods and the import of items never before seen in this country. As the price of coal fell and new industries and businesses appeared, energy prices dropped so the people benefited from reduced heating bills.

These man-made waterways became extremely busy and thriving, with constant relays of horses pulling along the carrying companies' boats laden with their cargos of coal, limestone and iron, leather goods produced in one of the area's most successful industries, barrels of locally brewed beer, and flour from local mills such as Pratt's Flour Mill, a tall canal-side building with tiny windows that were always coated with white flour dust.

Canal building in this area began in 1768 and continued until 1863, just short of a century producing 160 miles of canals, all located inside an area of around 220 square miles – a truly vital element of the prosperity of the region.

....

It was during the war years when we left the house on School Street to live in Leckie Road, and I remember having to walk all the way from the Wisemore to the new house, right through the town, along Stafford

Street, trudging past the shops and houses, clutching the hot water bottle Mom had made for me, holding it as close as possible and trying to ignore the damp, icy air clinging to my face and legs. Past the King's Head pub on the corner where Wolverhampton Street crossed with Stafford Street, past Hortin's greengrocer's shop with its wicker baskets of fruit and veg outside the front, perched on top of wooden crates by the curved Victorian window.

I hurried the whole way but it was such a long trek and all because we didn't have the penny for the bus fare! We never had any money for anything but my dad always managed to have his fags and booze, no matter what. He would even leave us with nothing to burn on the fire when he gave our coal to Mr Blower in exchange for a packet of ciggies and bottles of beer.

> Walsall had fallen into a state of depression through the 1920s and '30s, with industrial recession and a high level of unemployment: in August 1938 there were over 7,500 people out of work.
>
> The war brought economic growth to the area with essential war work ordered by the Ministry, and local industry began running at full tilt once more. So many different things were needed: Shannons made military uniforms; Patterson & Stone produced leather flying helmets; Helliwells carried out repairs to military aircraft, and T. Partridge & Company Limited manufactured gun shields, machine gun brackets, gun pedestals, ships'

winch casings, brackets for tanks and parts for the Scorpion tanks that destroyed mines – and even parts for Bailey bridges.

By the August of 1940 the unemployment figure in Walsall had fallen to just 533.

Many air raid shelters were made in Walsall as well, with Walker Brothers producing the Anderson shelters and T.Partridge & Company Limited making the Morrison shelters, as well as fixing up the damage caused to local factories that were hit during the bombing campaign. Although a lot of buildings were hit, there was only one air raid on Walsall Borough that took the lives of local people, when a single aircraft attacked the William Bate Limited factory on Hospital Street.

With the constant fear of air raids now, shelters began to appear all over the place and families who were on a very low income were given one free, so these strange little structures were popping up in back gardens everywhere. Very odd, they were – often the front was just a shaped piece of corrugated iron sheeting with a little oblong doorway cut out, and they would be covered with sand bags or earth, even grass and plants if you wanted your shelter to blend in with the garden! Some were very basic but people who could afford to do more with them would have bunk beds inside, heaters and lights, and a store of tinned food.

There was a shelter just across the road from our house, next to where a lady called Elsie lived. Mom had spotted that there was someone actually living inside and she went to see if whoever it was needed any help.

She found a woman called Claira Jackson, who had nowhere to live and she had her little baby girl, June, with her. She did have two boys as well, Richard and Leonard, but they had been put into a nunnery in Worcester. Claira Jackson had a very bad story to tell. Her husband had been violent and abusive to her and the children, so she ran away from him. When Mom saw this poor woman's plight, she just had to offer to help, and so Claira and baby June moved in with us. Later, her boy Leonard came to us as well: Mom would take him everywhere with her and she looked out for him. Claira, although still not with a man of her own, had another baby while they were living with us. A little girl, Carol.

I remember all too clearly when Mom wasn't at all well. They thought she'd gone down with the 'flu. Whatever it was, it hit her hard and she was right poorly. She had to take to her bed, which just wasn't like Mom, no matter what. I used to go down to a chemist shop on Stafford Street to fetch her medicine that they made up specially for her. It was a mixture of liquorice and chlorodyne, and a bottle cost half a crown: that was a lot of money in those days. Chlorodyne was made from laudanum – that came from opium – cannabis and chloroform. When she took the medicine, it knocked her out, good and proper. I was scared.

I wasn't used to seeing Mom like that. She wasn't getting any better and they found out she had

TB. Tuberculosis. A deadly disease that's been around since ancient times, and it attacks people all over the world. A nasty illness that makes you spit blood, gives you bad fevers and a dreadful hacking cough. It spreads very easily between people – someone only has to cough or sneeze, or even just speak near you, and you can catch it. Just like that. I couldn't stop worrying.

They took Mom off to Goscote Isolation Hospital, a special place where they only dealt with infectious diseases, such as diphtheria and typhoid, and one building was just for the patients who had TB.

> Originally Goscote Hall Farm, in 1920 Walsall Council bought the farm and the surrounding land because it was an ideal place for an isolation hospital – a project that had been talked about since before the First World War.
>
> The building work was carried out by William Kendrick & Sons, starting in 1928 and at a total cost of £17,995. The hospital was officially opened by the Mayor of Walsall, Mr E. H. Ingram, on the first of April, 1930. The separate building, with twenty-two beds specifically for TB patients, was opened in 1933 and the name was changed to Goscote Hospital in 1949.

It wasn't a place for treatment, it was for convalescence. In Mom's case, it didn't do her any good and she was moved to Pelsall Sanitorium, where the treatment was more therapy than medicine.

Originally the stately home of the Charles family, Pelsall Hall was a three-storey country manor house with tall chimneys and even taller trees surrounding the building like a frame around a picture. An important part of the therapeutic treatment was fresh air and lots of it, so the big wooden doors were kept open all of the time and the patients could breathe in the lovely clean countryside atmosphere. All of the patients were fed a healthy diet and were given regular exercise.

It all sounded really positive. But now I wasn't allowed to visit Mom any more.

This was the turning point in so many ways, none of them good ones. With Mom gone from the house and me never seeing her at all, Dad turned my childhood into a living nightmare.

GROWING UP FAST

The housework was tough, but it wasn't a problem. I didn't mind having to do it all because I was doing it for Mom, for when she came home. Trying to get Dad's clothes clean after he'd been down the pit was hard as hell, and bear in mind that back then there was no washing machine, no tumble drier, no fancy products to remove stains and ground-in dirt. There was good old-fashioned elbow grease and carbolic soap. All I could do was scrub and scrub, and hope that some of the black filth was actually coming out. It hurt my arms and hands, and I ached a lot, but I just got on with it.

It was the other side of our new life that I hated, and I couldn't do anything about it. I just had to put up with it. And I did.

As well as making me his skivvy around the house, my dad started to do things to me that no father should ever do to his child. As soon as I walked in the front door after my day at school, he'd grab me and force himself on me. Or I'd be standing at the kitchen sink, peeling the potatoes for tea, and he'd suddenly grab me from behind and overpower me. He was always there, always stinking of the fags and beer, and that musty cinder smell of the coal pits. He was a big man, broad and strong, and wicked to fight off.

Next thing, I'm having a baby. His baby.

I'd started school when I was four. St Patrick's Catholic School. And now I was fourteen. Every year at Christmas, all the pupils would go to the priest's house next door to the school building, where they would all be given an apple, an orange and a shiny new penny. This particular time, I was upset when we got back to the classroom and the nuns were asking me what was wrong. I heard myself telling the Mother Superior about what my dad was doing to me, how he was always forcing himself on me. I was glad I told her, because the nuns took me into their care and looked after me until the baby came. I hadn't even known I was pregnant.

When my time came, I was taken to the Walsall Manor Hospital in Pleck Road, and my baby boy was born there. I called him Richard. A few weeks later, they told me he had died from gastric problems. Poor little lad, gone before he had a life. The family, every last one of them, ganged up on me, calling me all the bad names under the sun because I'd had a baby out of wedlock and at my young age. They had no idea what the truth was and I was never going to tell anyone about what my dad had been doing to me all that time, and how it was his baby. So I said I didn't know, and they called me even worse for being a slut. Even when the nuns made sure he paid for his wrongdoing and he was given a prison sentence, they wouldn't believe anything I said about him. They hated me but I hadn't done anything wrong.

1945, Tuesday the eighth of May, the end of the war. Suddenly, the streets were filled with so many people celebrating, people laughing and dancing. Union Jack flags flew everywhere, garlands were hung from windows and folk were bringing tables and chairs out of their houses for street parties. The blackness that had been hanging over us for so long was gone, and it seemed everyone was happy again.

1946, Mom passed away from the TB sickness.

Dad married Claira. I knew they had been carrying on while Mom was still alive, and that Carol was my dad's child, my half-sister. Claira said she went with my dad to keep a roof over her head and make sure her kids were safe and fed. When Dad was put away for what he'd done to me, she found out and she said I should have told her before she wed him. I don't think that would have made any difference and I despised them both.

I was sixteen now and started my first real job as a sewing machinist at Shannon's Mill in George Street, a thriving four-storey factory that stood for the success enjoyed at the time by Walsall as a centre of industrialised clothing manufacture. But I wanted – and needed – to get away from Dad and Claira, and to make something of myself to prove I wasn't the waste of space the family had labelled me. So I applied for a nursing job at Walsall General Hospital on the Wednesbury Road.

> The General was always known locally as Sister Dora's Hospital because it was originally founded as a training hospital – the first of its kind – by a nursing Sister who became famous for taking care of cholera and typhoid patients during an epidemic, and when a mine shaft collapsed in a local disaster, she worked tirelessly and without a thought for her own safety to help the survivors.
>
> She was so well known and respected for her selfless efforts and the support she gave to her local community that there is a stone statue of her standing in Walsall town centre.
>
> Sister Dora was the first non-royal female to have a statue made in her honour.

Not only did I join the fine profession, but I was given lodgings in a staff dormitory where I shared a room with a girl called Kathy Spinks. Finally, I was freed from my sorry home life.

LIFE, DEATH, AND HOPE

I worked on Lion Ward and it was hard but I loved it. In those days, nurses didn't just tend to the patients: we would cook if one of them needed to be fed, and we did the cleaning as well. It was worse when there was an accident or other emergency, or someone else's shift had to be covered, and Matron would get us out of bed at all hours of the night. I looked after a lady I've never forgotten, a Miss Beck. I remember she was a twin. She had this big growth on her face that made breathing and sleeping very difficult.

Sister Day asked me to cook some sturgeon in milk for Miss Beck and help her feed. Because the milk had stuck to the pan, I left it soaking in the sink. Sister came stomping on to the ward and demanded to know why the pan hadn't been cleaned. I explained that it needed a soak first and that I would do it as soon as Miss Beck had eaten her fish, but that wasn't good enough. Sister stood and watched me trying to scrub the burnt milk off the pan and she wasn't happy with my efforts. She shoved me away from the sink and sent me flying into the fridge, dropping the pan and all the water splashing all over the floor... I picked up the pan and swung it, bashing her over the head!

She screamed at me, "You're fired! You're fired!"

But I went off to see Matron and told her what had happened. I was well in with her because she would always send me to Dennis Kempton's shop to get cigarettes for all the nurses. I had to go round the back and knock the door because cigarettes were still on ration, but Matron was courting Dennis so he was very generous to us. One day the police raided his shop and found a lot of pornographic books that Dennis kept under the counter. Matron finished with him there and then.

A few days after this, when I was back at work, I saw that Miss Beck wasn't in her bed on the ward and I asked Sister where she had gone. Stifled to death, she told me, choked by that awful growth on her face. I was shocked, and really upset to learn of the poor lady's passing, especially in such a horrible way, but Sister just told me rather sharply to get on with my work. I think this sad news got to me more because I hadn't been allowed to see my own mother when she died, and now someone else who I had come to care about had passed away before I'd had a chance to say goodbye.

Another upsetting time I remember clearly was

when there was a really nasty accident near the Malt Shovel pub on the Birmingham Road and a young couple were rushed into the hospital. The girl had been very lucky, with only minor injuries, so she was treated then sent home, but things weren't quite so good for her boyfriend, who was hurt badly. The poor lad had to have his leg amputated.

The next day, his girlfriend came to see him but, instead of spending time with him and comforting him, she callously told him she couldn't be with him any more, and then she gave him his engagement ring back. It shocked me to see how thoughtless and uncaring she was, and when she'd left it was heartbreaking to see him sitting there, propped up on his pillows, just crying and sobbing, not to mention in a lot of pain after the surgery – so I went over to sit with him for a while and chat.

That was it. Once again, I'd got on Sister's wrong side and she called me out for another telling-off! She seemed to be forever in a foul mood and I did eventually find out why that was. Her husband was the hospital chef and he would regularly take advantage of his position to mess around with the young nurses; he was always groping female members of staff while he was cooking their meals. It was common knowledge. I once heard a right commotion coming from the kitchen and when I went to see what was happening, there was Sister going hammer and tongs at one of the younger nurses, who, it turned out, was pregnant by Sister's hubby. I stood there gawping in disbelief as Sister battered her unfaithful spouse with a couple of pans from the stove. I did wonder if she'd learned that from me! The poor pregnant girl was shipped off to stay with the nuns until her baby was born.

....

When Dad was eventually released from prison, he went back to Claira but she threw him out and he ended up in a hostel.

Kathy Spinks and I started palling around together and one night we were out when this chap, Mr Arrowsmith, took a proper fancy to me. Whether I'd wanted to or not, he had his way with me and I couldn't do anything to stop him. Before long, there I was again, pregnant because some man had forced himself on me. But what to do about it? I had no idea where I could go, what would happen, so I just kept quiet about it for a few weeks, hoping to God that something would work out.

One time when me and Kathy were walking up Bloxwich, having a smoke, this chap shouted across the road to us, asking if we could spare a ciggie. He came over and we got chatting. His name was Ron and I was pretty taken with him; he must have liked me, because we started meeting up regularly and soon we were a proper courting couple. Of course, I had to tell him pretty sharpish about the predicament I was in, having Mr Arrowsmith's baby and all.

Ron did no more, but asked me to marry him

and said he'd take the baby on as well! We were saved, me and this fatherless baby. I know Ron went to see Mr Arrowsmith to tell him to keep well away from me and the baby when it came, and he gave the bloke a good thumping into the bargain, to make sure he understood.

MARRIAGE AND MOVING

On Saturday the fourth of November, 1950, Ron and I were married by the Reverend Parsons in St Peter's C of E church on Stafford Street in Walsall. I was twenty and Ron was just eighteen. Claira's daughter, June, and my half-sister, Carol, were my bridesmaids and our dresses were made by a German lady who was lodging with Claira at the time. Now we were Mr and Mrs Ronald Ray Stanton!

I gave up my nursing job and moved in with Claira for a while in Leckie Road. I made it clear that I wasn't going to be doing all the housework and skivvying for everybody in the place, and June wasn't happy with that so she shoved me down the stairs, with not a thought for me or my unborn baby.

From Leckie Road, I went to live with Ron's mum, Aida, on Parker Street in Bloxwich, and my new baby girl, Patricia, was born on the thirtieth of March 1951, fortunately with no ill effects from the fall. It was the time of the pitboy strikes and Ron was working on the local newspaper, the Express and Star, with his dad, who owned the newspaper print works.

I remember early in the morning of Wednesday, the sixth of February 1952, when my father-in-law was suddenly up and out of bed, shouting to Ron to hurry up and go with him to the factory, because the King had been declared dead and they needed to get this news out to the public without delay. King George VI had passed away peacefully in his sleep at Sandringham House.

> As a sign of the people's respect, Union Jack flags were flown at half-mast. The sad news spread and all sporting events around the country were cancelled, cinemas and theatres closed their doors, and no BBC programmes were broadcast except for news bulletins and the essential shipping forecasts.

The King is dead, long live the Queen!

The Princess Elizabeth, King George's daughter, was proclaimed Queen on the sixth of February 1952, as soon as her father's death was announced.

The following year there was a day for celebration like no other we'd ever seen, all over the country and even around the world.

> At 11.15 on the morning of the second of June 1953, the official ceremony for the coronation of Queen Elizabeth II began in Westminster Abbey. The BBC broadcast the whole service, all three hours of it, and the pomp and ceremony that followed. They told us that 27 million people in the UK watched it on television, and 11 million listened in on the radio.

It was the first time anyone was able to see such an important event on the telly and – even in black-and-white! – it was a breathtaking sight.

We were still the United Kingdom then, of course, and the Queen's bouquet, all pure white flowers, was made up of orchids and lily-of-the-valley from England, stephanotis from Scotland, orchids from Wales, and carnations from Northern Ireland and the Isle of Man. Her husband, the Duke of Edinburgh, looked so dashing in his full naval uniform, and what a handsome couple they made, travelling in the Gold State Coach, pulled by eight beautiful grey horses.

The wedding dress was straight out of a fairy tale, made specially by that famous fashion designer, Normal Hartnell, who used to make all her outfits, I believe. A vision of white satin, embroidered all over in gold and silver threads with the emblems of the UK and the Commonwealth, so even the frock made you proud to be a Brit!

Mind you, I wouldn't want the weight of that solid gold crown on my head, that's for sure! Nearly five pounds, it weighed! That's two and a half bags of sugar!

More countries than I knew existed, 92 of them, had their news reporters and photographers there, and one of them, a journalist with the Washington Times Herald, was a smart young lady called Jacqueline Bouvier. We never knew then but she would go on to marry John F. Kennedy, who became President of the United States, and she was his First Lady.

It was all so far from the life we lived, but you couldn't help feeling emotional. I wondered how many folk, all around this world of ours, would be tearful at the same time as I was snuffling into my hanky.

....

Aida exchanged the house on Parker Street for number 34, Shakespeare Crescent, in the Blakenall area of Walsall, because she needed somewhere with more space, with the family getting bigger all the time. Blakenall, which was also known as Harden, was part of the coal mining belt and was mainly developed as a council housing estate from around 1920, known as the Poets' Estate.

I was pregnant again by this time with Ronnie, we had Patricia, and Aida had sixteen children in all. Ron's dad fell ill and had to take to his bed with a condition called dropsy, which is basically excess fluid that makes the soft tissues swell up, and it was affecting him in his chest. So, as well as cooking and cleaning for everyone, I was nursing him as well, but I really didn't mind that because I really got on with him. While he was bedridden, I'd sit with him for a little while and chat, but Aida, who'd never liked me and never would, accused me of being "great" with him, meaning I was having sex with him, when the poor chap was laid in his sick bed, barely able to move.

Our Ronnie was born on the twelfth of November, 1953, and it wasn't long after that I fell pregnant again, this time with George. Ron's dad's sickness got worse, and you could say it was a blessing when he passed, even though he was only in his fifty-ninth year.

Before the poor man was cold in his grave, Aida disappeared for weeks on end, leaving me to do all the housework and cooking, and look after all the children, and when she eventually turned up again, she had a new husband in tow, a chap called Sammy Hillback – and his four kids from a previous marriage! He didn't know Aida had all her kids until they were wed and he came to live at the house. That must have been a bit of a shock for him!

Aida was always treating me bad, even though I'd never done her any harm, and she would bully me and shove me around all the time. She pushed me down the stairs while I was carrying baby George and I went into slow labour. I had to go to the hospital, so Ron's eldest sister, Patty – big Pat, we called her – was left to look after little Patricia and Ronnie. Aida decided she didn't need me any more, and anyway she'd just brought another five folk to live in the house, so she threw us out. Me, Ron, Patricia, Ronnie and our new baby, George – all out on the streets, and right after I'd given birth.

Ron went to the Salvation Army barracks for the homeless on Green Lane and I took Patricia and Ronnie with me to the Beacon Lodge workhouse, on the corner of Pleck Road and Moat Road. This place used to be the Old Central Union Workhouse until

1929. I had no choice but to leave baby George with Claira until we could get sorted out.

Even though Aida had thrown us all out and made us homeless, she made Ron pay her every week out of his wages from the newspaper business, which now, because his dad had died, had passed to Ron as the eldest son, so at least he had work. I had to do jobs for the nuns at the workhouse, doing laundry, cleaning the steps and other chores, to earn our keep for me and the two little ones. They did let me go to Claira's every day to feed little George, so I did get to see him and have a cuddle for a while.

Ron had been telling his grandma, Adeline, about our situation and she told him to go and fetch me and children, and we could all go to live with her and his granddad. So we moved in with them and Ron's brother, Albert, Adeline's sister, Betty, and her husband. With us, that made ten people in all, so it was overcrowded but that was normal for the likes of us in those days.

I used to go to the post office for Adeline's husband, Granddad Southall, to collect his war pension of half a crown, his dues because he'd been a prisoner-of-war in a German prison camp and had his fingers blown off. While he was held captive, a German doctor carried out some experimental surgery on his injured hand, inserting sinews taken from a dog into his arm. He never did get the use of his hand back and he always wore a big gauntlet to hide the damaged hand.

One time when I was out fetching the pension

money, me and Granny Southall were in the butcher's shop up the top of the marketplace buying a joint of meat, when little Patricia suddenly ran out of the shop and shot straight across the road. She ran straight into a local bobby and fell over, and one of her sandals came off. Granny Southall went mad at her but the copper asked her not to be angry because it was his fault, he said, even though we knew that wasn't the case. He picked Patricia up and planted a kiss on the top of her head, then he took a shilling out of his pocket and gave it to her. This was when my Ron was very well known to all the local police because he was always using his fists on somebody or other around the town.

Granddad Southall had been awarded the Victoria Cross from his time served in the army. This was the highest award given to members of the armed forces for gallantry in action against the enemy, and truly something to be very proud of. There was an almighty row in the house after it came to light that Ron's brother, Albert, had stolen the medal and sold it to buy fags and booze. What an awful thing to do to such a lovely old man who'd fought for his country. I can't say if it was anything to do with the upset from this, but not long after that, Granddad fell really poorly.

Adeline was getting a bit unsteady on her legs, and she was finding it all too much with the kids around the place so she asked Aida if we could move back in with her again. There was no bad feelings at all between us and Adeline, it was just for the best. Ron and I both adored her and Granddad Southall and we'd been very happy living with them, so it was a real shame that it had to come to this.

More than a shame, it wasn't at all a good situation because Aida carried on being dead nasty to me every chance she got when Ron wasn't around. Then, when he'd come back to the house and I'd tell him what she was doing, she'd try to turn it back on me, saying I was lazy, or dirty, or anything she could think of to find fault, to blame me for the arguments – even though none of it was true. She treated Ron the same as she was with her other kids and they all had to run about after her and do everything around the house, but her new hubby's kids did nothing at all to help out.

Ron's brother, Brian, had sneaked into the local picture house and seen an advert for the armed forces, inviting new recruits to apply and showing what a good life they would have. To Brian, this was too good to miss and he decided he wanted to join up; all he had to do was get the application forms from the local paper, the Evening Dispatch, but he knew his mother would never entertain the idea, with him being only fifteen and all, so he came to me for help. I saw how much he wanted to join up and I agreed to do what I could for him. Brian contacted the paper and they sent the application forms out in the post, so I had to make sure I grabbed the morning post before Aida could see anything, otherwise the game would be up. Even when Brian had filled the forms out, there was the big problem of having to get Aida to sign it to show her consent, and when I asked her about it she just refused point blank.

So I played a bit of a trick on her. I folded the forms over so you couldn't make out what was on them, and then I waited until I reckoned she'd probably put the matter out of her head and I went to her with the forms, telling her they were something to do with us trying to get our own house – so she signed, of course. I put the forms in an envelope and took them down the post-box.

Two weeks later, Brian went to Wolverhampton to find out if he had passed the tests he'd taken as part of his application, and it was good news. He'd passed on both physical fitness and knowledge. Next thing, he was being signed up to join the navy. The poor lad was over the moon and he never stopped thanking me because that changed his life and gave him a much better future than he would have had. I was happy for him.

One person who definitely wasn't happy, however, was Aida. She never forgave me and she made it her life's mission to cause as many arguments between me and Ron as she could. Life became hell again.

Claira went with me to the Housing Department on Hatherton Street in Walsall to see if they would give us a house of our own. The man behind the counter told me to go home and have another baby then go back and try again. As it happened, I was pregnant again, this time with Mickey, a new brother for Patricia, Ronnie and George. Back at

Aida's, I had to tell her the bad news and that seemed to get her all fired up again, causing even more trouble for me all the time. But, thank heaven, things were about to change...

I was up a ladder, painting the walls in one of Aida's rooms, when there was a knock at the front door. It was Mr Gayle, the cruelty man, as he was known. First off, he told me I shouldn't be climbing a ladder in my condition, then he said he'd had a report that the children were being neglected and he needed to inspect the house. I took him to see the beds, the kids' clothes and things, then into the room where they were all sitting round the table with their bowls of stew that I'd just put out for them. He was obviously satisfied that the children weren't suffering and they were fed and cared for, and he did let me know it was Aida who'd made the complaint but he could see for himself that there was no truth in what she'd been saying.

I think he felt sorry for my situation, looking after Aida's lot as well as my own, and working – while she was off up the town, drinking and having a rare old time of it. Then he said it was obvious that we were overcrowded so he was going to do what he could to sort a house out for us. I didn't hold out much hope, but, true to his word, he came up with the offer of a place – number 8, Farringdon Street in Walsall. The building was condemned, as everyone could see by the big bright yellow sticker on the front wall! The windows had all been put through and it was a bit of a wreck, but I didn't care about any of that because it was a house, a home. Our own home.

We got moved just as baby Mickey was about to arrive, almost before the putty had dried around the new panes of glass in the windows. Three bedrooms and two downstairs rooms, all to ourselves – this was luxury to us! I didn't even mind the one outside toilet that was shared by the whole terrace. On one side of us there was a lady called Mrs King; Mrs Jones lived just along the entry way, and at the end of the row was Mary Kale's shop, and everyone was friendly with each other, all helping out when anyone needed a hand. It felt just right.

There's always an exception to every rule, as we all know, and this was a family over the way from us who obviously thought they were better than the rest, too good to have to live among the likes of us common folk, and their kids weren't allowed to mix with the rabble, as their mother called us. A few weeks after we moved in, my best friend, Nancy Clarke, came to live next door, so I felt even happier and more settled. It seemed life was finally being kind to us.

I have to admit I always had a bit of a problem when it came to standing up for my kids, and when some lads were taunting my boy George over his bit of a speech problem that meant he couldn't pronounce his R's properly, I saw red and dashed out to give them all a slap on the legs. Straight away, their mum appeared, shouting and threatening me, so that was it – we started scrapping right there, out in the street! My timing couldn't have been worse because Ron was just on his way back from doing the papers so he grabbed me and dragged me off the other woman, throwing her back to her own house. As soon as we were indoors, he scowled at me and said, "Woman! You want to learn to behave yourself!"

I could always fight for my kids but when it came to sticking up for myself I was pretty useless. As for Ron telling *me* to behave, it was him who was up to no good, bedding any floozy who took his fancy. He started an affair with some tart named Doreen – she called herself Dee Dee – and one time when he got back home from being with her, he chucked a packet of tablets at me, saying, "Here, take these – you'll be needing them."

"Why's that, then?"

"'Cos I've picked something up off somebody, that's why."

TWO YEARS TOO LONG

I always knew one day Ron's fighting, and thinking he was above the law so he'd get away with it every time, would jump up and bite him on the backside, and it did. He'd got into some brawl or other and threw a hefty punch at the wrong person. Pat Gavin's jaw was broken. The really bad news was that Pat was a police officer. Ron had to go to court and they gave him two years in the nick.

While he was inside, he arranged with certain people for them to keep an eye on me and the kids. I guess that was so I didn't get up to no good with anyone else; after all, two years is a long time to be left on your own. One of these 'spies' was Brian, Mrs Jones' lad, and he did a good job of it, popping round now and then to make sure I was managing OK. Trouble was, he was so nice to me and the family, so kind and thoughtful, I started to feel attracted to him and I saw straight away that this went both ways. We grew close and it turned into a real relationship. I fell pregnant and Brian told me he wanted us to be together properly and that he was happy to take on all the children – Patricia, Ronnie, George, Mickey, Derek, Brenda, and the new baby that was on the way, the one he was father to.

Maybe because Ron had kept letting me down so much, or maybe now I just wanted something better, but, whatever the reason, I was happy and couldn't wait to start this new life with Brian. But we never stood a chance. Brian's mom knew exactly what would happen if we got together: when Ron was released he would have gone for revenge and Brian would have ended up on the wrong side of Ron's violent streak. God knows how that could have ended up. Next thing I knew, Brian's mom sent him away somewhere – I didn't know where – and then, in the blink of an eye, he was wedded to some woman. I was left having another baby, a little boy who arrived on the eighth of April 1961. I called him Brian after his dad and I really believed I'd be able to keep him. On my next visit to the prison, Ron just said, "I want that bastard gone."

Ron's release date finally came round and he was back home. As he was getting ready to go off and meet his mates, no doubt to entertain them with tales of his time inside, he just snapped at me, "I want that bastard out of my house when I get back."

I knew it was pointless trying to argue with him and I had to face giving my new baby up. But who to?

Claira knew a couple who wanted a baby and she fixed it for me to meet them. This navy officer chap and his Chinese wife came to the house and it all happened so quickly, no chatting or anything. I'd bundled up baby Brian's clothes and toys for them to take, but the lady just took him out of my arms and walked out, leaving the sad bundle where it was. I was left standing there, with no baby and just this pathetic pile of his little belongings to remind me of the child I was forced to give away so I could keep my husband. I heard later they changed his name to Trevor, after his new dad.

That was a measure of how much I loved Ron. Not just loved – I worshipped the man.

Ron had already been thrown into a terrible state of mind by something else that had happened while he was away. Aida and Ron's brother, Sammy, had only gone and sold off the newspaper business behind Ron's back, taken all the money from the sale and pretty much spent the lot. So, when Ron got out he had no job and no money. With our family depending on him to keep a roof over our heads and food in our bellies, Ron started thieving – but only so he could put meals on the table. He would rob meat from the local slaughterhouse and when we'd got what we needed to feed us, he'd sell the rest so we could buy other essentials. It wasn't that he was a thief by choice, it was sheer bloody necessity to keep us alive.

It had hit me really bad when I had to let the baby go, and I'd have these fits of misery when all I could do was cry and sob my heart out. Don't get me wrong, I've never been a softie, it was something way out of my control that came over me and I couldn't fight it, no matter how hard I tried. The vivid memory of that Chinese lady walking out of my house carrying my innocent little boy was tearing me to pieces inside. Of course, Ron couldn't stand seeing me like that, breaking my heart over another man's child, and he had his own way of dealing with the problem...

TIMES ARE A-CHANGING

Although I'd never told him, Ron must have sensed that I had genuine feelings for the baby's father, and it made him real mad when I was upset about giving little Brian away. He would lose it, good and proper. One time when he came back to the house and I was tearful, he snapped, ever so nasty, "I'll give you 'baby', woman! All this bloody crying around me!" and he grabbed me and forced himself on me, just like he'd done many a time before. That was Ron – if he wanted sex, it didn't matter a gnat's what I wanted or didn't, he'd take his pleasure anyway and it wasn't pleasure for me like that, just pain. And his anger.

I soon realised I was pregnant again.

Our house in Farringdon Street, the first house we could call our own home, was finally ready for demolition and we were given another new address, this time it was Number 67 Leckie Road in Walsall, where I gave birth to Sean Wayne not long after moving in. He was born on the tenth of April 1962, almost exactly a year to the day from when little Brian came into the world, so every year on Sean Wayne's birthday I was to be reminded of the child I had made out of love for his father and in the hope of a happier future. All dreams, all shattered.

More additions to our family came along while we lived here. Quite soon after Sean Wayne there was Diane, then Shaun, Dawn, and Nigel arrived in June 1971 – then I was sterilised so there wouldn't be no more.

Leckie Road was a good place for me, a place of friendship with like-minded females. Flory Barnes, Kathy Vaughan and Mary Stewart, or Irish Mary as we knew her. All good friends, all strong women, and we were living in different times now, a time when women were starting to demand rights and they weren't afraid to stand up for themselves – even if their men didn't like it. Yes, Leckie Road was good for me, but I can't say the same for me and Ron's marriage.

He started working on the fair at Bloxwich and I wasn't happy about that, seeing as I knew only too well how it was for the blokes on the fairground. They would pick up one girl after another because, for some reason, there was a fascination about the fair and the men who worked it. Fairgrounds are magical, exciting, loud and fast – and here today, gone tomorrow. Many's the girl been left carrying a fatherless baby to some swarthy, black-haired chap who gave her a smile and a wink. And more besides. I knew what Ron was up to, and things weren't good between us.

Sometimes, when the fair travelled away, Ron would go with them, leaving me to look after the house and all the kids on my own. To be honest, I was glad of the peace while he was gone, and it meant I could see Flory and the others whenever we fancied a chat and a cuppa. We really got to know each other during those times. Happy times.

Until the day Ron came home from one of the trips away and he was broken-hearted; something had upset him real bad. He told me the Bloxwich fairground site had been sold off for development and work had been started on digging up the ground to prepare for the start of the construction. He'd been asked if he wanted to help with clearing the rubbish away, only it wasn't rubbish. It was an awful, terrible thing. Shallow graves where children's bones lay, now unearthed and needing many questions to be answered. Who were these little ones? Why were they buried without ceremony or prayer? What had happened to them? Ron cried, real tears from this big lump of a man who'd knock seven shades out of anyone who looked at him wrong. It hit him so bad, it made him ill. I stayed up all night with him because he couldn't sleep without the terrors hurling him back to reality, making him see those tiny bones, over and over again.

BAD THINGS HAPPEN

Aida must have run out of other folk to stir up trouble for, because there she was again, having another go at me and mine. Mr Gayle turned up at the door just like before, but he didn't want to inspect or investigate anything...

He stepped inside the house and straight away reassured me, "Don't worry, I know these children aren't neglected. When I came to see you the other time, I was fetched by your mother-in-law and that's who's brought me here now. She's a nasty woman!" He asked me if my husband or any other man was living with me and the children, and I told him Ron was inside again. I thought he had a really kind face and I reckoned he'd seen a lot of bad situations that must have affected him. He could see I'd got my hands full, just like last time.

"I believe", he said, "you could do with a rest from all of this hard work and struggling on your own, and I can arrange for the older children to go on a holiday for two weeks with the church. Father Curtain will be in charge of everything, so don't worry about them."

And that's exactly what happened. I was so grateful, and quite shocked because nobody had ever done anything like that for us before. As well as organising the holiday for my eldest ones, he left a parcel of children's clothes with his wife for me to fetch, things that had been collected by the WRVS[1], and he told me to go to his daughter's house on the Great Sutton Road the next day to pick up a load of clothes and toys for the kids, that had belonged to his grandchildren but they'd grown out of. When I went to the house, Mr Gayle appeared from his place next door to hers and we had a cup of tea and chatted. He said if I ever needed anything at all, I should call on him. I never did, but I remember his kindness to this day. I wasn't used to it.

One thing I *was* used to, was having to make some pretty difficult choices, that's for sure, but sometimes the choice wasn't mine to make and that can be even worse. A chap we knew called Billy Walker had a sister who owned a shop that was stood empty at the time, and some of the kids got caught doing damage to the property. Unfortunately, our Ronnie was one of them and for his efforts he was sent to an approved school in Lichfield.

---

[1] **Women's Royal Voluntary Service**: Founded in 1938 by Lady Stella Reading as the Women's Voluntary Services for Air Raid Precautions.

The Beacon School, run by Walsall Education Committee, was a residential institution for up to 73 children who were *'mentally defective though educable'* and the impressive building had previously been the home of the Midland Truant Industrial School for boys, opened in 1893 to take in schoolboys who were persistent truanters.

The original school closed in 1924 when the building was bought by Walsall Town Council for £8,000 and was used as a sort of holiday camp for local children through 1925 until the new Beacon School opened its doors on the second of March, 1926.

These youngsters were subjected to a very strict military-type regime of education, work, exercise, recreation and early nights. And, if that didn't put a stop to their antics, corporal punishment was the next step.

Two of Ron's brothers, Johnny and Maurice, were sent to Beacon School because they wouldn't go to school, then our Georgie joined them, but only because of his speech problem, not any wrongdoing on his part. I agreed to him going there so they could help him learn proper speech: I hated to see him taunted by the other lads about the way he spoke. Kids can be so cruel. The brothers kept absconding from the school and turning up at our house, and Ron would have to keep taking them back again. I didn't mind his younger brothers seeing me as their mom and I'd look after them, seeing as their own mother wasn't really capable.

I was in the garden, getting the washing off the line one time, because I could see it was going to rain, when I spotted a pair of feet poking out from under the pigeon shed, so I called out, "Who's that under there?" I got no answer, so I shouted again, "I know you're under there so come out now!" Still nothing, and now it was pouring with rain and even that didn't make our intruder show himself.

When Ron got home, I told him to go and have a look in case they were up to no good, and he did. He took hold of the feet and dragged out a very reluctant Georgie, thick with mud and wringing wet. We got him washed off and dried out, into a change of clothes and put some food in his belly, then his dad said, "Come on, son, I'm taking you back now."

The poor lad ran to me and clung on to my legs, crying and pleading with us not to make him go.

"Please, Mom, I don't want to go back there... please don't make me!" He was starting to get a bit hysterical so I asked him whatever was the matter. He just said he was scared to go back but it was clear there was something else he wasn't telling us, so I left him with Ron and took myself off into another room, hoping he'd open up to his dad. It worked. He told Ron the hairdresser at the school had been "doing things" to him. It didn't take Ron long to realise our boy had been sexually abused.

"Woman, keep him here with you, he ain't goin' back there." Ron's face was enough to tell me what he was going to do, and I didn't blame him. He stormed off to catch the bus to Lichfield.

When Ron arrived at the school, he demanded to see Mr Pete, who was the owner of the place, and said he should fetch "that nonce hairdresser" with him. As soon as Ron clapped eyes on this bloke, he thumped him, knocking him spark out. Mr Pete sent for the police and Ron held his hands up, but he made sure they listened to the awful things he'd had to hear from our frightened little boy. "And my boy ain't comin' back here, never again!"

After the police had investigated, and some of the other boys had revealed similar accusations against the hairdresser, it turned out he'd been abusing the youngsters when they went for their haircuts, when he was on his own with one lad at a time, then he'd give each of them half a crown and a bag of sweets for keeping quiet, for protecting his filthy dirty secret. I know violence should never be an answer, but I was glad Ron hit him as hard as he did. He deserved far, far worse.

Ronnie and the others had no choice but to stay on at Beacon School because their time there had been Court ordered as punishment for playing truant, but Georgie was sent to a special education school, Castle School in the Leamore.

> The Castle School was a new building designed with lots of big windows to allow light and an airy atmosphere with good ventilation. The building work had cost £53,000.

49

It was the first special school in Walsall and had only been opened in September 1959, taking in children aged eight to sixteen, with eight classes of twenty children each. Instead of being a place of punishment and correction, this was a school specifically for children with special needs, with teachers who had experience in this work and a head teacher, Miss Aline Sabin, who had previously been part of a remedial teaching team in Wolverhampton.

This school was kitted out with specialist equipment to provide visual and practical instruction for the pupils, who would all have been given a Statement of Special Needs and would experience moderate learning difficulties, although most of them would have additional issues such as autism, speech and language difficulties, and behavioural issues.

So this was a far better place for Georgie with his speech problem, and I was much happier with him there.

That hairdresser was taken to court and given a prison sentence, then we heard that Mr Pete's family was struck by tragedy when their new baby died. Mr Pete had been carrying the newborn down the stairs when he fell and the baby was sadly crushed to death under the weight of its father. This was more than the poor man could deal with, and soon after that he and his wife moved away from Walsall. I hope that helped them recover somehow, but I'm not sure folk ever mend after such a dreadful thing.

ME AND MY KIDS

Over the years, I started to feel weary. Not just weary from the hard work as I grew older, looking after all the kids and the house, and worrying about what bother Ron or the boys would get into next, but tired – oh, so soddin' tired – of Ron's affairs. One after another, sometimes more than one on the go, and nothing I could say or do was going to stop him.

The more he kept going off with his cheap tarts, the more I felt I couldn't keep on fighting for him, arguing and rowing with him, then thinking I'd won him back for good, only to find out he'd got another floozy lined up somewhere. So I made the children my life instead of Ron. He could come and go, but me and the kids would be together through whatever life threw at us. I knew there would come a day when Ron wouldn't be able to carry on with his womanising, and then he'd settle down. I could wait.

Maybe it was this stronger relationship with my children that made me even more protective, I don't know – it could have been the frustration of being married to an unfaithful husband whose other main hobby was causing punch-ups and getting into bother with the police – but I found myself getting into fights of my own, as daft as that sounds now.

It was when we lived in Leckie Road I had most of my brawls, always over one or another of the kids. Jeannie Tapper was one of our neighbours and her boy, Billy, poor lad, had a glass eye. All the kids were out in the street eating ice cream and suddenly all hell broke loose. Our Mickey came running in the house, shouting for me so I dashed outside to see what was going on, to find Jeannie shaking our Georgie, who was crying his eyes out.

I saw red, of course. I grabbed hold of her, dragging her away from Georgie, and I battered her. Just like that. I broke her nose. Billy was trying to get me off his mum as we grappled in the gutter, so I gave him a few good slaps as well. Unfortunately, his glass eye fell out and started rolling away down the street. Blood running down her mouth, Jeannie staggered to her feet, shouting all sorts at me.

"Why don't you go get yourself knocked up again and 'ave more kids? I'm sure your hubby can manage it, 'cos he's knocked up half the street!"

I just had to retaliate. "Ain't it about time you got a bloke to marry you, so you can stop livin' in sin and your kids won't have to be little bastards?"

Another time I remember, I sent Patricia out with her little friend, Colleen, to fetch some coal in the wheelbarrow Ron had made specially for her. Not long after they'd gone, Colleen was back, all upset and shouting that some man had "got Pat and showed her his thing!"

I called across to a neighbour to keep an eye on the kids and ran with Colleen to where Pat was, still with her barrow and still with this idiot man standing there. Colleen pointed to him. "That's him, Mrs Stanton! 'E 'ad 'is thing in 'is 'and!"

I squared right up to him, ready to punch his lights out. "What the bleedin' 'ell d'you think you're up to?"

"Nothin', missus! 'Onest, I ain't seen these kids before!"

Colleen called him a liar. "You fetched your dinky out to Pat!"

He stood there, with his haversack on his back, so I pointed to the ground and barked at him to take it off. "Put it down there."

As he bent down to put the bag on the pavement, I dived on him and set about him, thumping and kicking real bad, until he broke free and ran off. Then I picked the bag up and chucked it into the middle of the road, where it stayed until I'd left with the girls and put some distance between us. It was only then he dared go back for it!

I was even more mad with him because Pat had lost the money and we still had no coal.

Our Mickey needed some new baseball boots, so I took myself off to Emery's, the draper's store. It was one of those shops that sold a real mix of things and I decided, seeing as I was there anyway, I'd pop upstairs to have a look at what they'd got in the way of household bits and bobs. As I got to the top of the stairs, I saw Ron and he was with that slapper, Doreen, and her in that big grey fur coat he'd bought for her. Mutton dressed as lamb, she was. Then I spotted they were looking at dinner services and she'd just called him over to see some cups and saucers. He saw me. "What are you doin' in 'ere?" he snapped.

"What are *you* doin' 'ere, you mean? And what's her fuckin' doin' 'ere?" I was fuming.

Ron squared up to me. "Get down them stairs now!"

"I've come to fetch my lad's shoes and that's what I'm gonna do!"

Then Doreen chimed in. "Ron, come away from her. Come and look at these."

That was it. I was in such a rage and I just had to do it. I lunged at the stupid cow, grabbed her by the fur coat, and I gave her a real good hiding. Worst place to have a set-to, I reckon, a crockery department. Quite a few things went flying and got smashed. Ron caught hold of me and spat words at me. "Get yourself 'ome, woman – I'll see you later."

So I left.

The store people made Ron pay for the damages and he wasn't at all happy about that. When he came home, I did get a beating, but I reckoned it was worth it, just to give that floozy a thumping.

I found out why they'd been looking at dinner

things when Mrs Jones and Aida showed me an advert they'd seen in the local paper, "couple looking for flat" with some contact details.

When Ron came home that day, I chucked the paper at him. "What's all this about, then?"

"I didn't do that – it must 'ave been her."

Another time, when I was with Claira in the queue at the meat counter in Sainsbury's on Park Street, that bloody woman was in front of us. She turned round.

"Oh! oh, it's you!"

"Yes, it fuckin' is me! Ron's wife!" And with that, I grabbed hold of her hair and pulled her down to the ground, and I battered her, right there in Sainsbury's. Claira dragged me off her.

"Leave her, come away before you get yourself in trouble again."

Claira knew I'd get another hiding from Ron when he found out, but I just couldn't help myself, whenever I saw that man-grabbing bitch. I just had to have a go.

Next thing, Ron came home with some papers for me to sign.

"What's this, then?"

"Just sign 'em, woman!"

"Them's divorce papers!"

"I know, now just bloody sign 'em!"

"Will I bollocks!" And I ripped the papers to shreds and threw the lot in the back of the fire. Ron just walked out. I never really believed he wanted to be with Doreen, but she could never leave him alone.

Some time after that, Doreen got married to some chap, and I hoped things would settle down, which they seemed to – for a while, anyway.

Then, one night Ron came stumbling into the house in a right state, all covered in blood and clearly badly beaten. His white shirt was nearly all dark red, and the vest he had on underneath was soaked through. I got him out of his clothes and discovered he hadn't just been battered – he'd been stabbed. He wouldn't hear of going to the hospital, so I cleaned him up and saw to his wounds as best I could.

I found out later that Ron had still been carrying on with Doreen, but he told her he was finishing with her. That wasn't what she wanted at all, so she lied to her new husband, telling him a tale about Ron trying it on with her. He got some of his mates and they waited for Ron to walk by, then they all set on him. It was Doreen's husband who stabbed him.

When he'd recovered from his injuries, Ron went back to Doreen, just to show her old man he wasn't frightened of him and that he could still have her if he wanted – that made the bloke a laughing stock around town. To add insult to injury, Ron gave him a good beating in front of all his mates.

Ron was very well known in town, both liked and feared because there were two very different sides to him: he could be as nice as pie but he could be right nasty as well. You never really knew if you had him as a friend, but you knew sure enough if you'd upset him because the place would clear in seconds! He was a mad one, no two ways about it, and he never knew when to stop.

I put the kids in the pram and went up the Savoy picture house once, looking for Ron when he'd not come home with the coal he was supposed to be fetching. Doreen was working there so I knew that was probably where I'd find him. There she was, in her uniform lilac frock with a yellow tabard over it, and she saw me straight away. "You can get out of here, right now!"

"No, I won't – I've not come to see you, I've come to see my husband, Ron."

She tried to push me out of her way. I grabbed her and pulled her frock up over her head and right off, leaving her stood there in her bra and knickers. She threatened to tell Ron.

"Go tell your own husband, 'cos one thing's for sure – you'll never be Mrs Stanton!"

I was referring to the divorce papers that would never be signed, and letting her know that Ron hadn't pushed me for them.

Mr Hato, the Savoy's manager, must have heard the commotion and he came hurrying out with a face like thunder. "I'll have you done, so I will!"

"Go on, fetch the coppers! Why are you on 'er side? You fuckin' 'er as well?"

I knew I had to make a dash for it now. I rushed home, got the kids washed and put to bed, then

I hid in the outside toilet with both my feet wedged up against the door. Ron came home eventually and shouted from the house, "Woman! I'm gonna kill you when you get out of there!" So I stayed there all night, and even managed to get some sleep.

When Ron came downstairs the next morning, I was getting the kids ready for school. He just looked at me and shook his head.

And so, life went on. Ron with his affairs here and there, but always Doreen; me with the kids and the house. I knew he just wanted to have his cake and eat it, so I let him carry on.

I know I paint a pretty bad picture of Ron, but, as well as his real nasty side, he could be funny sometimes and act silly, make us laugh. But then, just as quick, he'd turn again and we'd all get hell. Like one time when he came in and I was cooking tea at the stove, veg all boiling in pans, and I had a knife in my hand for checking if the spuds were done. He came right up behind me and started teasing and tickling me, so I swung round and threw my hands up to stop him. The hot knife caught his neck and burnt him. He sent me flying across the room and started on at me with the usual barrage of abuse about my past.

"You had a kid by your own dad! And when I was banged up, you couldn't wait to get some other bloke in my bed!" and so on.

This was always the red rag to the bull. I went back at him. "What about you and all your cheap tarts? I bet you've lost count! I know I have!" And I'd remind him of all the different women he'd slept with over the years.

"You couldn't even keep it in your trousers with our Betty, your own brother's wife! How low can you get?"

Whenever I mentioned Betty, Ron would actually try to excuse what he did by saying, "I had to sleep with Betty 'cos our kid can't have kids of his own!"

As if that made it all perfectly okay.

LIVES. AND DEATH.

On the sixth of June 1971, or – as a later copy of his birth certificate states, the fifteenth of June that year – Nigel was born. He would be our last child and after him I had the op to be sterilised. Our Pat, by this time a young woman of twenty, an adult in her own right and married to Steven Powell, gave birth to her son, Craig, on the fourth of August 1972.

A month after Craig arrived, Ron suffered a massive heart attack and I was told he wouldn't survive. My ever-cheating husband had been with his bit of fluff, the one who called herself Dee Dee, the one he'd kept on seeing over the years, the only one that really got under my skin. She lived on Dartmouth Avenue and Ron was making his way back home from her place when he keeled over. People walking past saw what they assumed was another drunk, falling about on the ground, and they stepped around him and went on their way. He wasn't drunk, he was having a serious heart attack and it nearly killed him.

While he was in hospital, not expected to

recover, Pat took little Craig, Ron's first grandson, to see him and that seemed to perk him up a bit. From there, he grew stronger and eventually, against all the odds, he was allowed to come home, where I nursed him back to health, and life went on again.

Ron got back on his feet and, as soon as he was ready to take on a new project, he managed to arrange a haulage contract with National Carriers and bought a fleet of wagons that he rented out to the drivers who worked for him. One of these was a chap called Barry Reed, and he and his wife, Alma, came to live with us for a while. I loved how folk saw our place as 'open house'. So, we had money coming in again and everyone was alright. But Ron's affairs carried on, and I knew he was still seeing that Doreen.

Our family began to take on a different character, with all the kids growing up and making lives for themselves, making their own way, and making their own mistakes. Pat's husband, Steven, came to our house one day and told Ron, "'Ere, you can 'ave 'er back – she's been playin' away."

And so Pat moved back in with us. You always hope your kids will do better than you and it breaks your heart to see them struggle through the same kinds of hell that you hoped they'd never have to know.

Pat wasn't coping with baby Craig but she wouldn't let Steven or his family have the little lad, nor would she even let them help out with him, and, before we knew it, she'd arranged to have the poor mite adopted out. Next thing, social were at the door, and there was Mr Gayle with them, come to collect little Craig. I'd hid him out of sight and Ron told them they wouldn't be taking him anywhere. The lady social worker insisted that Pat had signed him over for adoption and so she said she had to take him. She made a point of saying that I wouldn't be able to take care of another child. As soon as her words were out of her mouth, Mr Gayle spoke.

"I know this lady and, in my opinion, she is more than capable of looking after all of the children, including little Craig." He'd stood up for me again.

And so it was agreed that Craig would stay with us, and me and Ron raised him as one of our own. Pat was always off with another new boyfriend, so it was for the best. Craig was happy with us and his dad would come to see him regularly and take him out for the day sometimes. Dawn would go with them because Craig had developed a really strong bond with her; he followed her everywhere and she was like a little mum to him. Of course, when Pat found out Steven was seeing their son, she was furious and told us she wanted him back, but Ron put his foot down and didn't let her take him.

It was much later, when Craig was seven years old, that Pat married again and she did take him back. I was heartbroken at losing him, but they only lived up the street in Keats Road, so I could see him whenever I wanted, especially as Pat was working now and needed me to take care of him. Pat could be very difficult at times, and whenever I didn't do everything she wanted, exactly *how* she wanted, she'd stop talking to me and not let me see Craig. She would argue with me, and fight with me, and I'd be the one ending up in tears, but later she'd be back on my doorstep when she realised she needed my help again. It was a really stupid situation, but that was Pat. And that's how things went between us for years, until we had the fall-out to end all fall-outs.

I saw our Ronnie get married to Viv, Mickey to Kathy, and my kids all started to fly the nest. It wasn't so easy for young Georgie, though, when he set up home with his girlfriend, Doreen Jakes, and they had little Michelle, then she took off with Georgie's friend. Some friend, I thought. Georgie couldn't handle it and he tried to escape from it all with drink and drugs, no doubt desperate to blot out the childhood abuse as well as this rejection from the woman he loved – and losing his daughter. He fell into a dark world and spiralled out of control. It was so hard to see him like that.

Alongside the heartaches, the family was growing all the time with grandchildren and I loved them coming round to visit. It made my day to see their little faces and they knew I'd always have some treats waiting for them. Why wouldn't I? I was their nan.

Since Ron's heart attack in 1972, he had bouts of illness at times with his heart, and then he was diagnosed with diabetes, but I always nursed him every time he was took bad and he'd get back on his feet again. He had to have a heart bypass more than once and I knew he needed serious help or this was going to go a bad way. I found out about an Egyptian doctor, a consultant cardiothoracic surgeon at the National Heart Hospital in London, who was famous for performing many successful heart transplants and he was also known for his belief that, if someone needed his help, he should give it. I wrote him a letter asking if Ron could have a transplant. I got my wish and Dr Yacoub operated on Ron, after which his health picked up real good.

No matter what Ron's health issues were at times, he never once stopped seeing Dee Dee, and over the years she had two children by him, both girls.

Shaun's partner, Wayne, lost his mom in 1996 and I took him under my wing and loved him like he was my own. He was always such a lovely lad to me, and the three of us spent a lot of good times together, shopping, day trips out, bingo and such like.

It was 1998 when Ron took ill again and this bout lasted a good twelve weeks. I knew he was real bad this time. And then, just like that, he was gone.

It was the lung cancer that took him, and I was by his side, right up to when he drew his last breath.

Without me knowing, Ron had organised with Shaun to arrange his funeral and he'd said to make sure it was the basics, nothing fancy, nothing that would cost much. He'd left his money to me so I'd be alright; it was his way of showing that he loved me – heaven knows, he was too damn stubborn to show me when he was alive. The house he left to be passed on to the kids when I'd gone.

I couldn't let my Ron go to the next world without a proper send-off, so I changed all the arrangements. A horse and carriage instead of the hearse, dress suits hired for all the boys, and I got a friend who had a voice like an angel to sing Mario Lanza's 'I Walk with God' in church. People came from all over and we did Ron proud. I just wanted to show how much I loved him.

My Ron, the man I'd loved above everything, the man I'd always forgiven for his terrible ways, no matter how much he hurt me... he was dead. I loved him and I hated him for leaving me and the family, but now I couldn't even tell him.

ON MY OWN – THE AFTERMATH

After we lost Ron, everything changed. People all deal with death in different ways, but what happened in our family was more than that: it was like all of my children were going off the rails, falling out with each other, falling out with me, and they all had their own issues that they didn't seem able to cope with.

Nigel started hitting the bottle, and his heavy drinking got worse and worse; Sean Wayne wasn't sleeping and couldn't stop crying all the time; Diane was spending way too much time up the cemetery, driven by guilt and unable to forgive herself because she had wished her dad dead, and the others just drifted, like they'd got no meaning to their lives. It was breaking my heart to see my children so lost, but I wasn't in the best of health now and I was carrying my own grief, too.

Our Georgie went down a very bad road, losing himself in the drugs and drink, and even ending up in prison because of the things he did to his wife when he got into a real bad state. When he came out, he was supposed to stay with Diane but she changed her mind and he had to go into the Good Shepherd Church hostel in Wolverhampton.

Dawn was doing her best to help him but she had me to look after, and her little boy, Charlie, had to be her main priority. Georgie turned up at my place a few too many times, as high as a kite, having promised my Ron on his deathbed that he'd never touch the drugs again.

So I could keep my eye on whoever came to the door when Sean Wayne was off doing God knows what, leaving me on my own in the house, Dawn had bought me one of those CCTV set-ups and this was especially useful if it was Georgie and he was high, because people can be unpredictable when they get that messed up.

He'd had his orders to keep away but I just had to ring him now and then to check how he was – after all, he was still my son, drugs or no drugs, and I'd get Sean Wayne and Nigel to go check on him sometimes. A mother can drive herself insane, worrying about her kids who get into those ways.

Sean Wayne had got Georgie a job making fence panels for a mate of his, John somebody, to keep a roof over his head and put some food in his belly, but John apparently caught him with drugs on him and sent him packing. Trouble was, Georgie had got money in his bank account and those undesirables he called friends started to take advantage of him for their beer and drugs.

I had the police turn up at the door one day when I was in on my own, so I got them to phone Dawn to come round. She came straight away and the coppers told her Georgie had been found dead in his flat, some pokey place he'd found in town. They took Dawn off into another room and she told me later they'd said they were investigating his death as suspicious.

After that, Dawn was in contact with the police and she found out they had evidence that Georgie had died somewhere else and then been taken back to his place, propped up in a chair and just left there. Toxicology tests proved he did have drugs in his system, and this was confirmed by the Coroner. We were asked if we'd like to attend the inquest before Georgie's body could be released.

Dawn and Nigel went to the Coroner's office in Wolverhampton and the details of their brother's death were explained to them. Three other people were involved, so it appeared – a couple called Diane and Dave, and their son, Craig. Craig had been found dead inside a rubbish chute in some block of flats and his parents had upped and left town.

The investigation uncovered that Georgie had been drunk and, while he was asleep or unconscious, someone had injected heroin between his toes.

The police could have tried to track down the missing couple, but that would mean Georgie's body would have to be withheld as evidence, so we couldn't bury him. The option was to leave the case with an open verdict, then we could go ahead with the burial.

Dawn and Nigel could see I was distraught, and because of my Catholic faith, I needed to give my son a decent burial without such a delay. It was agreed we'd accept the open verdict. After all, finding that couple wasn't going to bring back our Georgie, was it?

I wanted to have him cremated and his ashes laid to rest with his dad, but Sean Wayne insisted that he shouldn't be put in the ground because of his drug abuse, so I gave in and bought a cremation plot in the cemetery where Ron was, so at least I could visit them together.

Dawn saw how things were and she started coming to see me every day, bringing her little boy, Charlie, with her. That cheered me up no end. She could see how much her dad had been helping me because I could only get around on my sticks or in a wheelchair: bless him, he'd get me showered or washed, he'd cook the meals and generally take care of everything and make sure I was looked after.

Dawn wanted to do whatever she could to help out and she would take me shopping, sometimes meeting up with people she knew, or we'd visit friends at their house and have a cup of tea and a chat, and sometimes we'd stay at her house and sit together and talk, mother and daughter. Rather than leave me home on my own, she even took me with her to her evening cleaning job at the bookies, so we could chat while she worked. It all helped me, especially because it got me out of the house; Dawn wasn't at all happy with me being there because Sean Wayne had taken over the whole house and even the outside area, and he had some of Ron's old trucks, cars and bits of cars and engines, wheels and tyres and all sorts of tools and metal contraptions all scattered around the place. The garden was nothing more than a scrap yard. It was bad, I knew that, but I didn't want to leave – it was my home, the home I'd shared with Ron.

Dawn asked me many times if I would consider moving in with her and Eric; she kept pointing out how filthy and unsafe my place was now, especially seeing as I couldn't move around easily. She was worried.

Unfortunately, because the house was in my name now, when the state of the place was brought to the attention of the local council, I got a court summons that said I was cutting up cars in the street and causing all manner of environmental problems, breaking loads of rules and regulations. Even though it should have been obvious to anyone with half a brain that I could barely cut up a loaf of bread these days, so it couldn't have been me doing these things, not by any stretch, and it was really Sean Wayne, I still had to go to court. First, it was magistrates' court and then Crown Court, to face the charges. Says a lot about our justice system, I reckon. Diane stepped in and the judge decided to have some of the wagons and bits of old cars removed, and get the place cleaned up a bit. I tell you, I was shitting myself in case they put me in the nick!

We'd got into this routine of me being with Dawn all day and she'd feed me lunch and tea, and really look after me. She wouldn't leave me at my place unless Sean Wayne was at home and every night when she finished her cleaning job, we'd drive to mine and there'd be no sign of him. Many's the time poor Dawn had to drive around, with little Charlie wrapped up in a blanket on the back seat – and him with school the next day, poor lad.

Dawn would drive from one place to another, looking for Sean Wayne, trying everyone she knew who was a mate of his, until we'd eventually find him. I'd shout at him to get his backside home pretty quick so Dawn could get Charlie back to hers and into his bed. She even bought Sean Wayne a mobile phone so she could get hold of him to save us driving all over the shop, but sometimes he'd answer it and other times he wouldn't. He really wasn't being fair on his sister or anyone else. Very often she would have to take me back to her place and get her other brother, Shaun, and his partner, Wayne, to sit with me until she could track him down. I'd lose my rag with him.

"Where d'you think you bin this time?"

He'd answer, "I bin on business – if there's cash to be made, I gotta go."

Whenever Diane, Pat, Shaun, Nigel, Brenda or Dawn would have words with Sean Wayne about him giving me and Dawn the run-around, he would give me grief after they'd gone. He often left me in bed on my own, he'd switch the heating off in winter (even though

I was paying the bills), and his tools and bits of engines and stuff were piled up and littered all over the house, including on the stairs, making it really difficult for me to get up and down. I had to use the first floor bedroom because the room on the ground floor that was supposed to be my room was full of engine parts and it was filthy dirty with oil and grime, leaking batteries and the like.

No matter which one of the others tried to make him see sense, nobody ever got anywhere with him. They'd shout at him, they tried ignoring him, and sometimes they'd threaten him, but Dawn would always bite her tongue and walk away because she knew he'd never listen. It was so upsetting. I'd be sitting there in tears, and I'd say, "I'm gonna go into that care 'ome over the road! I'll be better thought of in there."

And so it went on, year after year for ten years in all, and then I realised the sense of it and I moved in with Dawn and Eric, and their boys, Charlie and now little Harry as well.

Even then, some of my kids just couldn't be happy for me; they had to cause trouble, no matter what. Diane got herself banned from Dawn's house for her meddling and stirring, then Dawn fell out with Pat over this and that...

Dawn had had enough of the lot of them, especially when it came to the subject of Derek having sexually abused her when she was little, and some of the others had been putting their two penneth in, even though they didn't know the true facts. She decided she was going to talk to the police about the abuse, and the awful things Derek had done to her back then. But, before she did anything, she wanted my blessing and she asked me if I was okay with her doing this. I told her she should do what she felt she had to do, and I wouldn't mind.

"I know how you feel," I told her, but at that time Dawn had no idea that I had my own story of abuse in my family.

This was the skeleton in the closet that was about to tear the family further apart. Shaun and his partner, Wayne, stood by Dawn, Diane suddenly jumped on board and announced that she had been abused by Derek as well – this was the first I'd heard about it. Pat stopped talking to me, Craig stopped talking, Brenda disappeared, so did Mickey, and Derek stopped visiting with his disabled son. It was all such a mess. I didn't blame Dawn because she was doing what was the right thing for her. I know what it's like to be called a liar or told you're crazy when all you're doing is telling the truth. I should know.

Dawn said the police were going to talk to everyone in the family to find out what each of them knew. I had decided before this, when I was still living at Greenrock Lane, that I would do the right thing by Dawn and tell the police I had known what Derek was doing to her when she was a little girl, but Sean Wayne told me not to get involved, that I should let Dawn and Derek and the others fight it out among themselves. He said if I started talking, the police would keep coming back round to the house and that wouldn't be good.

I was caught between the devil and the deep blue sea, because Sean Wayne was the only one I still had with me and I was scared he'd go and I'd be left on my own. There was no way I could have managed.

So, when the police had turned up at the house that Saturday morning while Sean Wayne and Brenda were there, and they spoke to us all together, I'd kept my mouth shut, just like he told me to. Scared of my own son, that's a terrible thing to admit. I wish I'd told the police that I *had* known about it, because one of the other boys had caught Derek in the act. It could have all been sorted back then, but I was too scared.

I'd carried that with me over the years, knowing what a son of mine had been doing to my little girl, and now I was dreading Dawn asking me if I had known. But she never asked, bless her. I couldn't bear the thought of falling out with her, so I told a bit of a fib and said I'd told the police I could only remember Dawn coming to me at the time and telling me that Derek was doing things to her. I felt awful about that, because it was like I was doing exactly the same to her as my family did to me all those years ago.

Dawn was proved right about the state of the house, when I had a pretty nasty fall on the stairs. I was trying to go up to bed and Sean Wayne's big spanners, wrenches, car jacks and so on were all over the stairs, so I couldn't get a proper footing. I missed a step and my hip gave way, sending me tumbling back down and falling on all the piles of metal. I knew I was hurt bad but I couldn't make a fuss. Sean Wayne rang Dawn and she turned up real quick with Shaun and Wayne; Dawn held the wheelchair while Shaun picked me up and between them they got me into the chair.

I refused to go to the hospital, stubborn old fool that I was, and I couldn't move so I sat there all night until Dawn came back in the morning with Harry. Sean Wayne had gone out and just left me there in the chair. Dawn told me I looked ghastly but I asked her not to tell anyone and not to call a doctor. But then Diane arrived – she'd been driving past and spotted Dawn's car outside – and she commented as well.

"Mom, you look really grey, what's the matter?"

Dawn kept quiet but little Harry chimed up, "Nanna told Mommy not to say anything 'cos she fell down the stairs."

Diane rang for an ambulance. She and Dawn had to carry me – still in the wheelchair – through the house, over all of the metal obstacles and general rubbish, and down the driveway to wait for the ambulance. Had it not been for Diane that day, I reckon I could have died from shock.

It was while I was laid up with my broken hip, Shaun was took with a stroke, leaving Wayne, who was poorly himself with that lung ailment – COPD[2] they call it – caring for him. Shaun had several more strokes after that, but then, unbelievably, Wayne had a stroke

[2] COPD: Chronic Obstructive Pulmonary Disease – a group of lung diseases affecting the breathing, including bronchitis and emphysema.

himself, so then Shaun was trying his best to take care of him. It must have been like something out of a book or a film – you couldn't make it up.

Wayne started to get better, thank heaven. Shaun couldn't stop worrying about me and Wayne as well, and he ended up having a complete breakdown. Harry went to stay with them to help out, especially since Dawn couldn't be there for them because she was looking after me. What a bloomin' mess we were all in!

I know Dawn wanted to keep it from me that the boys were in such a bad way, but they lived close to her so it was impossible to keep me in the dark for long, and anyway, I could read them all too easily, so I knew something was up. By the time I did get the facts, they were both recovered, so I didn't have to worry quite so much.

Nine weeks I had to stay in hospital, and Dawn and Diane stayed with me, night and day. I had a hip replacement and eventually I was ready to go home, when a social worker turned up and told us they needed access to my house. Dawn told her she wanted me to live with her because my house had been turned into a death trap: everyone agreed – except Sean Wayne, of course. Dawn said the others could all visit me at her house and so it was agreed. I moved in.

MOVING ON

The kids all visited for a while but in time they stopped coming, all except Diane and Sean Wayne, and he was always on at me to go back to Greenrock Lane, and he'd sit there crying, telling me he was going to fetch me back. I was torn because I felt safe and happy at Dawn's, like when I was at home with my own mom, but I felt sorry for Sean Wayne, having to live on his own.

In the summer of 2009, we found out that my boy, Ronnie, had taken really ill. The worst of it was that he'd been bad for some time but didn't tell anyone, just kept it to himself.

Suddenly, he was being told he had lung cancer. He and his wife, Viv, were led to believe there was hope for him to be treated, but within a matter of weeks he had a lump biopsy taken from his leg and after that he couldn't get around at all.

Dawn would take me to visit him and he'd be in bed or lying on the settee, completely unable to get up and move about on his own. He would cry to me and that really upset me, seeing him so ill and weak. Broke my heart, it did.

His condition got worse and he was admitted to Stafford Hospital. It wasn't looking good. Ronnie wanted to go back home – he must have known he hadn't got long left and wanted to be with Viv in their home, not in some hospital ward with folk he didn't know. But the nurse in charge of his care told him he had to stay where they could monitor him.

After a while, probably because there was nothing more they could do for him, it was agreed that he could go home. He was in a real bad way by now, so very poorly.

The ambulance arrived and pulled up on the driveway, but Ronnie never made it into the house. He died in the ambulance. The poor crew weren't sure how to deal with the confirmation of death because this had never happened before.

Dawn left me with Pat for a while and she drove round the family, picking them up and taking them to say their goodbyes to Ronnie.

Viv arranged everything for the funeral and Ronnie was cremated. His ashes were scattered at the war memorial in Cannock Chase. I wasn't happy about that, because I had nowhere to visit him or take flowers.

From admitting he was ill to drawing his last breath in September 2009, it was just six weeks. No time at all. And another of my children, gone before their time, before me. Rest in peace, Ronald Samuel.

....

2010. My 80th birthday was coming up on the eighth of March. Dawn organised a party for me, inviting all the kids, and when they were gathered together she announced that I was living with her now, for good, and anyone who was causing me any stress was *not* welcome. She also made it clear to them that I would no longer be handing out cash to them like I'd been doing. Sean Wayne had been bringing me all the bills for the house and I was paying them – phone, electricity, water, and I'd give him money for shopping, too.

From here on in, things started to get nasty. Dawn would ask Sean Wayne to visit me when he'd cleaned himself up a bit, not filthy from messing about with the engines. Diane would tell him he shouldn't be claiming carer's allowance because, not only was he not looking after me now, but he never had been! Anyway, she told him, I wasn't even living at the same address as him any more. There was so much bickering going on, but the girls did have good reason.

Christmas, 2013. Dawn was in the kitchen and Diane had just told Sean Wayne again about having no right to claim carer's allowance. He got up off his chair and went to hit Diane, and I started crying – when was this all going to end? Dawn came striding into the room and told them both to leave. Sean Wayne stormed out but Diane stayed to help Dawn calm me down and get me into bed. A bit later, Dawn's neighbour called to let her know she had a flat tyre on her car, and in the morning Eric checked it. The tyre had been slashed.

Dawn phoned Sean Wayne and told him, in no uncertain terms, to stay away and never come to her house again. Of course, no sooner said than there he was, banging his fist on her window and shouting about being my carer and taking me back home with him. Why couldn't he just see sense, that I was much better off with Dawn and Eric? I have no idea. But I suppose it was mainly about the money.

All the while he was outside, ranting and raving, threatening Dawn with all kinds of things, and I was getting more and more upset, and telling Dawn I didn't want to go with him, but I asked her if maybe she could let him start coming to visit me again. Next thing I knew, the coppers arrived and that got me even more agitated, but Dawn reassured me that she'd asked them to come round.

Sean Wayne was striding around, shouting his mouth off.

"I don't know nothin' about no tyre! I'm my mom's carer so that gives me every right to go in this house to see her any time I want!"

Then he flung round and pointed at Dawn. "Her's crazy, tapped in the 'ead, she is!" But Dawn stayed calm, bless her, and she just repeated to the police that she didn't want Sean Wayne in her house causing all these rows every time he came near. She looked at him and said, "Slashing tyres is one thing, but lies is something else, and you're not welcome here any more."

I felt torn in two, sorry for Dawn having to put

up with all the fighting and carrying on, when she and Eric were just trying to do what was best for me. But Sean Wayne was my boy and I was sad for him, being in that big house all on his own, knowing he didn't really manage by himself.

The next day, Social Services turned up to see me. Yes, it was Sean Wayne who'd rung them and told them all sorts of rubbish about how Dawn was treating me real bad. They asked me if I wanted to see him or Diane, and I told them I did but best not to have them at Dawn's, so I said I'd go to them. It wasn't the best arrangement for me, and Eric could see how unhappy I was, even though I tried my best to hide it, and he spoke to Dawn.

"I can't stand to see the duchess so upset, bab. How about we let them come back but I'll have a word with them and tell them they need to start behaving themselves in our house?"

Dawn agreed and the two rebels were told there was to be no fighting or arguing, especially in front of me.

The first time Sean Wayne came round, he just couldn't help himself, could he?

"I told ya you couldn't keep me away from my mom!"

I was so fed up with his attitude, I snapped at him, "Keep it buttoned and stop being so gobby! I've had enough of all your shit stirring! I'm an old woman now and all I want is some peace and quiet. Is that too much to ask?"

Things calmed down. But not for long...

Dawn and I soon realised that, no matter what we said, nor how many times we said it, the others just seemed incapable of respecting anybody else's wishes or needs. They didn't even seem to understand that I was an old lady who just couldn't take all the shouting and rowing any more.

Diane kept turning up, trying to cause arguments all the while, and Sean Wayne would arrive at Dawn's around nine o'clock at night, then he'd sit there until the early hours – without a thought for Dawn and Eric, and it was their house he was in! Dawn had to be up with the two boys for the school run and Eric had an early start with his job. They didn't need this disruption in their lives, and it was all because they'd had the good hearts to take me in.

I felt I could talk to Dawn these days and I started to open up to her about the family. I'd kept telling them I needed a quiet life now but they were so selfish, they just kept on doing whatever they wanted, trying to start rows and fall-outs between themselves. I'd grown so tired of it all and I really could do without it. So could Dawn.

"I'm so sick of the lot of 'em. I thought by now they'd know 'ow to behave, but no chance of that!" Dawn knew I meant it.

Sean Wayne was now into his fifties and he'd asked Dawn to tell me he'd got himself a girlfriend. First off, we were told she was his age, then that changed to her being in her forties, then she was suddenly thirty-something. Course, it turned out in the end, she was pregnant and in her twenties! He brought her round and I took against her straight off, but Dawn would try to get me to see there was a good side to this situation.

"Think about it, Mom. He's got someone else in his life now so it won't be that bad for him when anything happens to you. You can stop worrying yourself about him." She was right.

But I kept my distance from this young woman and it wasn't long before I caught her out in her lies. She told me her dad owned the gun shop up the Walsall market, but I knew the chap who really owned it, and he weren't no father of hers, that's for sure. I'd worked out something else as well.

I told Sean Wayne, "That's not your bab she's carrying, is it, son? Your mother might be old but she's no fool – but *she* thinks I am!"

I couldn't take to her but she had two boys and I loved them to bits. It wasn't their fault, what their mother was. Sean Wayne was coming round all the time now, him and her sitting with me at Dawn's, and him telling her all manner of tales, laughing and joking about things, like the time somebody gave him and Ron a microwave and they sold it to me for thirty quid. Course, Sean Wayne blamed Ron for that, now he wasn't here to argue. I knew what they'd done and I never found it funny. He joked about all the times he'd driven Ron up to see Doreen, and that really hurt me because I was always so close to Sean Wayne but I'd never known anything about that.

After they'd gone, I was really upset and I told Dawn, "I don't know who's the worst of them two – Ron or that son of ours. I've always been treated like a fool but I never expected it from him, not Sean Wayne."

The next day, Dawn had a word with him, telling him how much he'd upset me by talking that way about something so painful to me, and him making such a joke of it all. He still didn't get it.

"Me dad said her could turn the tears on when her wanted."

This latest insult showed me that Sean Wayne had not one ounce of respect for me, and I knew I couldn't keep taking the hurt and his bad ways. Nor could Dawn and Eric.

March, 2014. Dawn told me that she reckoned the best thing for everyone would be for us to move somewhere new – and not tell the family. I agreed. As much as it was a sad, sorry thing to have to do, I had to think about my health and peace of mind, which I was never going to have with them carrying on like they did. I really was worn out with it all. Anyway, Sean Wayne had been relying on me for way too long now, and it was time to stop.

We decided to tell Shaun and his partner, but nobody else. I asked Dawn if she'd ring the others later, "Once we've gone, so they don't come up causing any more trouble", and she said she would, just to let them know we'd moved and that everything was alright.

NEW START

Moving to Cannock took me back to our first few days in Farringdon Street, where all the neighbours came over to introduce themselves and give a hand, and to offer cups of tea. This felt like the same friendly atmosphere, the same feeling of a real community. Everyone made time to stop for a chat, so you got to know the folk around you and everyone was there for each other.

The new place needed a lot of building repairs doing on it, so Dawn and Eric had their work cut out for quite a while, but, as a home, I couldn't have had better. It felt calm and peaceful, and we made it a happy home.

It was a busy life, too, with all the work going on, Dawn taking me to see those family members we didn't want coming to us, and regular visits from Dawn's friend, Angie, Shaun and Wayne, Carol, Viv and Brenda, all taking their turn at looking after me.

The weekends were lovely times together, with shopping in town and the many day trips Dawn would plan for us to enjoy.

Shaun and Wayne spent a lot of time with me, taking me out and about, and they'd make up lovely bunches of flowers for me to put on Ron's and Georgie's graves.

Once a week, while we were doing the school run, we'd pop in on Sean Wayne and the boys, or we'd meet up in town and go somewhere for a bite to eat. Everything seemed to be turning out nicely, and I was settled now – and very happy.

....

2014. One of the family said my son, Trevor, had been in touch with them, trying to find me. Dawn and Brenda made arrangements for us to meet for a meal, and it was a stressful time because this was the first that most of them, Dawn included, knew of his existence.

Dawn got in touch with the others to break the news, and their reactions were all very different. Mickey said he didn't want to know, but that he was happy for me; Viv said Ron had told her about Trevor but she had never known if it was true or not; Penny wanted to know why nobody had told her she had another uncle; and Sean Wayne, true to form, asked if we wanted him to "see him off".

"Nobody's seeing anybody off!" Dawn told him.

"That's what Mom had to do over fifty years ago, so now it's all about what Mom wants in her life."

....

Time moved on and I started to feel ill, not right at all. Dawn had me straight to the doctors for check-ups and they did a scan on my stomach. We were waiting for the results.

Having enjoyed this phase of a quiet life at the new house, we heard from Social Services that they'd had a report of Dawn abusing me. Here we go again. I was so upset, and even more so when I discovered that it was Diane and Sean Wayne who put the report in. I was in tears every day and I could see Dawn was worried sick at how this was affecting my health.

I managed to pull myself together when the social workers came round to interview me, and I asked Dawn to fetch a letter our Diane wrote to me when I'd fallen out with her.

"I'll crack a bottle of champagne on your grave, you've already killed one son," she had written, referring to George. I showed the social workers the letter and told them it was from Diane, and I also told them she was the one who abused people because she had hurt me.

"I'm sure she's trying to kill me." I don't think they took me seriously, but I just had to say it, because it's how I felt.

The social workers left, saying they would be in

touch again, and I couldn't stop worrying. Why couldn't Diane and Sean Wayne just get on with their own lives and leave me be? The worry got me down and I wasn't sleeping properly, didn't really want to eat, and my mood seemed to swing between dreadful anger and couldn't-care-less, and I was tearful a lot of the time.

I even stopped doing my puzzles and magazine competitions, that Dawn had kept buying for me after I had a memory test, to keep my mind active. Even my knitting, that I was always so busy with, was sadly neglected. I could see all of this worried Dawn, but I couldn't pull myself out of it.

After a few weeks that seemed to drag on for months, a social worker called to say they hadn't found anything at all to support the so-called report of abuse, and they told Dawn I'd been most insistent when I spoke to them about what I wanted, and that all I wanted was to stay with her and Eric. They asked Dawn to tell me the news but she said – and she was dead right – that I'd think she was just trying to pacify me, to stop me being upset, and so she asked them to tell me themselves.

They did, thank heaven, and I can't explain just how much better that made me feel in an instant. I started eating more, sleeping better and life was good again.

We managed to keep things nicely settled until September 2016. It was actually on Dawn's birthday when the phone rang and, when she had finished speaking to whoever it was, she said we had to go to the hospital because a friend of hers had had an accident.

Leaving me in the car with Brenda, she hurried in and it was only later that she told me she'd really been to see our Nigel in there. He'd been blind drunk again and had a bad fall, breaking his arm and hip, but Dawn had checked on him and said he was going to be fine after some treatment.

"I knew something was up," I pretended to scold her. "I can read you like a book!" I also knew she hadn't told me straight away because she knew I would only get upset and have another sleepless night. That "reading like a book" worked both ways, obviously.

Dawn took me to the hospital, where we met up with Brenda and all went to see Nigel. As soon as I saw him, I knew he was going to be OK so I didn't have to worry. The doctors were going to start him on a detox programme to get him clean of alcohol before they could operate.

While we were all sat round his bed, chatting and trying to lift his spirits, his partner, Kay, made an appearance, being wheeled in by a nurse. Even though just visiting, she'd been put in a wheelchair because she was alcoholic, the same as Nigel, and they wouldn't risk her falling or hurting herself while on hospital premises.

These two were totally dependent on each other, but in a bad way. They were destroying themselves and each other through the drink. Kay opened her bag and started pulling out some of Nigel's clothes and Dawn asked her what she was doing.

"So he can come home." But Dawn wasn't going to sit by and allow that to happen.

"Come home? But you're both homeless because of the drinking being more important than keeping a roof over your heads."

With that, she took Kay's arm and walked her out of the ward, saying they would fetch drinks for everyone. Kay told her she'd had to sleep in the back of a van last night. It was truly pathetic.

They came back with drinks and snacks for all of us, and Kay was very quiet. Dawn told Nigel she wouldn't let Kay walk back to where she was staying, and that we would give her a lift, so we all stayed until visiting time was over. As we left, Dawn had a final word for Nigel.

"Do *not* leave here – or else! We'll come back later."

Once we were driving, Dawn spoke to Kay. "Nigel will be coming home with us when he's allowed out. If you want to get help with your drink problem, I can help you to get a placement."

Kay just muttered, "No... I don't want to stop."

Dawn was determined to sort Nigel out, whatever it took. "Okay, that's fine. If you want to kill yourself, feel free, but you're not taking Nigel with you. When we drop you off, I'm going to take his dogs, because if anything happened to them, it would destroy him."

True to her word, Dawn dropped Kay off and then got the two dogs into the car. As she climbed back into the driver's seat, she turned to me and asked, "Mom, are you okay with Nigel coming to live at ours?"

"It's your house, Dawn. I've lost one son to drink and I don't want to lose Nigel, because he's my baby."

We carried on visiting Nigel every day for the next month while doing the school run, and every day Dawn would tell Nigel that he would be coming to live with us.

Every day, the same answer. "I'll see, girl. I don't know yet."

But Dawn would keep going back with the same patient reply. "Well, I do know, because I'm psychic and I can see into the future. You are coming home, even if I have to drag you out of here!"

Because Nigel and Dawn were the two youngest of our brood, they were always close and he respected her for her straight talking.

The day arrived when Nigel was being signed out, and we went to collect him. Dawn had taken him something to wear, but it was only pyjamas. She laughed as she teased him, "No way will you be running off wearing these!"

On the way home Nigel said he'd thought he was going to be able to pop in to see his friend. "Your friends are at home," Dawn told him, "and you're not going to be dragged around by fools any longer." Nothing else was said until we arrived at the house.

Dawn and Eric had prepared so perfectly for Nigel's arrival: there was an electric bed, new clothes, shoes – basically everything he needed. It showed how much they cared and I think Nigel was quite touched.

"You live with us now. No fools, no drink, and I'm going to help you because if anything happened to you, it would kill Mom." She was right. I couldn't even think about what might have happened.

With the help Dawn and Eric gave him, and the support group she arranged for him to join, we soon started to see an improvement in Nigel, and he got better and better. The road to recovery.

STRUGGLING

The good news was that Nigel had come out of that dark place he'd been in for thirty years with the drink, and we were all grateful for that. The not so good news was that my own health had taken a bit of a dip again.

By November 2016, I was in the hospital every Thursday having treatment for pneumonia, a chest infection and iron deficiency. This was how things were, right up to Christmas.

Poor Dawn was knocked sideways, and she was physically and mentally drained. She'd done nothing but care for and sort out other folk – me included – for so long now, and hardly a moment to herself. A body can only do that for a time, then something has to give.

Happily, Nigel was in such a good place now, he was able to chip in and help. He'd do the cooking while Dawn was at the hospital with me, and he'd take his turn sitting by my bed all night. I really felt I'd got my boy back.

That Christmas came, and by then Nigel had been clean, alcohol-free, since the September, and no sign of him falling back into his old ways, thank heaven.

He did ask if he could go to visit some friends for new year and I was worried because it's that time of the year when everyone has a drink. I didn't want him to go.

"I'm not his keeper, Mom, and he has to be trusted some time." Dawn was right. You can't keep somebody a prisoner, you have to let them make their own way. And so, Dawn dropped him off at his friends' place and told him she'd pick him up later that evening. When she collected him, Dawn asked if he'd been drinking and he said he hadn't. "We'll talk later," was all she said.

She did speak to him that night and he admitted to having a can of Guinness, just to celebrate the new year. Dawn told him that was fine, but it was his one strike and there wouldn't be a next one. She warned him again that I was in hospital, fighting to stay alive, and if anything happened to him, it would take me really bad. I don't think I'd have survived it.

Nigel spoke to his support worker and he carried on doing well, going from strength to strength. Both Dawn and I were so proud of him. Thirty years is a long time to have something evil controlling your life.

Just into the new year, my condition got worse again and I had to have a blood transfusion. While I was in the hospital in Stafford, the consultant came to speak to me and Dawn. He wanted to do some camera tests on me to check for bowel cancer.

I was terrified at first, but, once I'd talked it all through with him and Dawn, I decided it would be the sensible thing to do, so I agreed. The consultant said I'd be fast tracked and everything would take about two weeks.

Dawn rang Sean Wayne to let him know I was poorly and she told him what the consultant suspected, asking him to keep this to himself until we knew more.

Almost a month went by – and nothing. Dawn complained to the doctor in Cannock Hospital and then we had a letter confirming details of an ultrasound, after which I was to have an MRI scan in the following weeks.

I had the scans and we waited for the results. And we waited. Again, Dawn had to chase and she was constantly phoning the doctor, who kept telling her it was on his to-do-list. I wasn't happy with this – it was like I didn't matter, I was old and therefore not important.

We changed to a different doctor in our area and put in a formal complaint about the other one. The next day, a letter arrived in the post. The MRI scan had revealed an aneurysm, and there were lesions on my liver. That would have frightened the life out of me, but they had compared the lesions to the scan I'd had done back in April 2016, and there hadn't been any change in size, so that was a good thing.

We tried our best to carry on with life in the normal way, back in the routine of shopping and coffee or lunch with various friends. While we were out one day, walking round the shops, some pals of mine came over to ask how I was doing because they'd heard I had the Big C. "Who told you?" I nearly shouted at them.

They all said the same thing. Sean Wayne. That boy would never change.

I got ever so upset and started crying, thinking that Dawn must have been keeping it from me, and that I really did have cancer. "No," she tried to reassure me, "I promise that's not true; they are just checking you out to see what's what. Nobody knows anything yet." Sean Wayne had managed to upset the apple cart and annoy his sister yet again.

Dawn arranged to see him and she tore him off a strip, so she did. She told him I was only having tests and check-ups and that nobody knew what I did or didn't have yet. "I told you to keep it to yourself that Mom was being checked out – why have you been telling people she's got cancer when nobody knows anything yet? We've got folk coming up to us in the street, asking her about it, and that's getting her upset again. You just can't help yourself, can you?"

My health was deteriorating and now I had become anaemic, so the doctor sent me to have the camera put down my throat – a procedure I was supposed to have had with the previous doctor, but I'd been left waiting.

Dawn took me to the hospital for this test, and Trevor came with us, seeing as he'd come up from Devon to visit me. The first attempt wasn't successful, so they put me on a fluids-only diet for the forty-eight hours before the next attempt, in the following week.

When I came out from the second test, I was on oxygen. The consultant told me and Dawn he'd found a tiny lump in my stomach and that he wanted to admit me to Newcross Hospital for more tests.

From less than a month earlier, when I was told the doctors thought I might have bowel cancer, then the MRI scan results saying there were "no concerns", it was like being swept up in a hurricane to arrive at them finding a lump in my belly and being taken in for more tests – and the consultant being concerned about stomach cancer.

Dawn updated Nigel and Brenda, then she took me to the hospital, where I was admitted for blood tests, biopsies and scans. It was now the middle of April in 2017.

Good old Dawn visited every day, and she could see I seemed to be getting worse all the time. I wasn't getting out of bed, I wasn't being fed, I'd become doubly incontinent (to my horror – that's not how you want to be, not in a thousand years) and I was drinking out of a plastic beaker!

Brenda, Dawn and Trevor were all trying to get some answers. Why were my basic care needs not being met? Dawn made attempts to speak to nurses every time she came in; she'd take photos of my medical notes, diet notes and monitoring notes, and she'd confront a nurse with these, but she was getting nowhere.

Once, when she read "missed meal off ward" on my notes, she challenged the nurse. "Why didn't you give my mom lunch again?" It was because I'd been having another scan when the food was brought round.

Dawn got so frustrated and angry at this apparent lack of care and communication, she demanded to have a meeting with the ward matron, so she could complain formally. In the meantime, she was asked to meet with the consultant and a specialist nurse, when she was informed that I did have stomach cancer – but it was a small lump. They explained what the options were.

Over the following days, however, this changed to "Your mother is too poorly to have any treatment" and Dawn couldn't cope with this. Nigel stepped up and he basically held Dawn together, keeping her going with his support and his words of wisdom.

Dawn got the meeting she had asked for, with all of the nursing staff in charge of my care. "My mom was not like this when she came in", she told them. "She could eat, walk, toilet and feed herself." I'm pretty sure they would have understood that Dawn was not happy with the way things had gone, and that she was telling them they hadn't done a proper job.

She also made it very clear that, although I was eighty-seven years young, I would have any treatment that was possibly going to help. Apparently, the only treatment now on offer was that I could have a stent fitted in my stomach, to allow food to pass through.

The doctor agreed, and I was to be transfused and prepared for the procedure on Thursday the twelfth of May, 2017, but they told Dawn I would need to sign a DNR (*Do Not Resuscitate* instruction) because my health was so poor. He also agreed that arrangements would be made for Dawn, Nigel and Charlie to see me on the morning of the op to help calm me, but this was also in case I didn't pull through.

This was another thing they got badly wrong, and, while Dawn and the others were on their journey to the hospital, I was already in the operating theatre. They were distraught, hating the thought that something could happen and they hadn't had a chance to see me. Dawn wanted answers.

Luckily, I made it! The plan now was for Dawn and the others to visit the rest of the family, tell them I had cancer and explain what the outlook was. We'd been told I probably had around four to six weeks left. This was based on the consultant finding that the cancer had metastasised. In other words that we can understand, it had spread.

Something happened at this time that I didn't know about, once again because Dawn and the others were trying to avoid me getting more upset, stressed, whatever, and that would affect my recovery. Wayne had a heart attack and had to go into surgery to have stents fitted, but the first I knew of it was when he was back home and out of danger.

It had been my decision not to let the family know I was in hospital and having the procedure, but now things were very different.

On the way home from the hospital that evening, Dawn, Nigel and Charlie stopped off to speak to the others, to give them the news. Diane's was first on their route home. She asked if everyone else knew, and Dawn explained that they would all be told that evening. Derek's was next but, just as Dawn knocked the door, one of his neighbours came out and told her that Derek's son had passed away

Then it was Sean Wayne's turn. As he kept his garden gate firmly locked so that no-one could get in, Dawn rang him. She'd hardly got the words out when he started having a go. "I'm getting a solicitor to come and see her at yours. I've got rights. And secondly, where's the grave deeds?" There followed a barrage of threats and insults, and Dawn just listened calmly until he'd finished. "Fine, do what you want, but you'll have to live with your actions when Mom's gone."

They went on to Pat's home. Standing on the doorstep, Dawn gave her the same message. "Mom's asked me to tell everyone she has cancer and it's terminal. And will you let Craig know, please?"

"Oh, Okay." The door was closed.

The last one to call on was Viv because she lived closest to Dawn's house. She asked Dawn, "Are you going to let everyone come to yours now, then?" Dawn replied, "Would you let the paedophile back into your home around your family?" "No." "So why should I?" Dawn turned and left.

AGAINST ALL ODDS

An ambulance pulled up outside the house at ten o'clock at night on the seventeenth of May, 2017. It was bringing me home. Me, my oxygen mask, tank and machine – what a palaver.

Then it turned out they'd given me the wrong dosage, so back I went to the hospital again, and spent the night sitting in the corridor of A&E until a new prescription was sorted. I was finally home again around three in the morning, with a different machine.

Dawn was upset because I was a bag of bones, and no wonder, with the meals I'd kept missing. I was struggling to breathe and I could see Dawn was scared, although she always put a brave face on. She and Brenda decided to look after me together, and Nigel would help, especially with lifting me in and out of bed.

The family members who I wanted to see were told they could visit, and Dawn kept the others up to date by sending them photos of me every day on their mobile phones. A lot could happen in a single day with me in this state.

According to the medical folks' prognosis, I was expected to be confined to bed now for the duration, I'd stay on the oxygen and I'd live on these drinks that were supposed to replace food, all full of vitamins and minerals – but not very tasty, and I'd have to be cared for by St Giles Hospice nurses and the district nurses. Anyway, that was their idea, but it wasn't mine.

In less than a week, I was eating by myself – okay, it was only blended food, but it was doing me good and it was all my stomach could take just now. I started taking a few steps with my walking frame, so I was getting to and from the toilet on my own, and then I got myself off the oxygen for most of the day, and – best of all – I could pick up my cup of tea.

Within a matter of weeks, the St Giles nurses and the district nurses asked if we were happy to continue without their day-to-day support, because they were so impressed with my progress. I told them it was because I'd got my three angels looking out for me – Nigel, Brenda and Dawn. This was great news and we agreed, so the visits were stopped and from then on we would have a weekly check-up over the phone. Dawn would get me to pose for a photo and she'd send that round all family and friends, so they could see how I was getting on.

One of these friends was Wayne Marshall, or Welsh Wayne, as I called him because we already had too many Waynes! He was an old work colleague of Dawn's who became a friend and he'd been a regular visitor when I was in the hospital, popping in every day during his lunch break to see how I was doing. When he got married, we went to the wedding to see him get hitched to his lovely wife in July 2016, and Eric said he felt like he was seeing his own son get married, we were all so close. Wayne used to call me Nan Doris and I liked that.

I'd tell Dawn often, "I'm not going anywhere, girl. I'm staying here to watch Charlie and Harry grow up and I need to keep an eye on Nigel as well."

I did know I'd got what they call terminal cancer but Dawn explained it to me very differently. She said "terminal" doesn't mean you're dying, no more than other folk are, it means you have to learn about your new ailment so you can live with it.

Hearing it like that did help me, and I think it made me stubborn enough to carry on. Things aren't like they were when my Ron was took by the cancer twenty years ago, and that was a different type of cancer from what I'd got.

It wasn't long before I started doing my puzzle books again, and I set to and knitted two baby shawls, twelve baby jumpers and one adult size jumper. It pleased me to see the garments taking shape and knowing someone would be wearing them.

We'd go off to the shops like we used to, to buy something new for me to wear, especially when I'd cashed in a winning scratch card; I loved getting new cards and couldn't wait to see if I'd won. Dawn said I was addicted!

I never used to be able to talk about death, but

recently I've been making arrangements for my own funeral, and for Nigel's, and Shaun's and his partner, Wayne's. It doesn't scare me any more – I even make jokes about it.

"They'd better have scratch cards up there, else I'll be coming back!"

SUMMING UP A LIFE

In my life, when I was still a child I lost my mom and after that my dad would have his wicked way with me all the time, getting me pregnant by him – even though I didn't know about things like that. The bab died. That broke my heart.

I married Ron, the love of my life, and he controlled me with his violence. He'd abuse me, too, when the mood took him, forcing himself on me, no matter what, but I still loved that man.

Some of my own kids have abused me in other ways, probably because it's what they learned from their dad when they were youngsters. After Ron was took by the cancer, I was so scared to be on my own, I didn't dare to upset any of them and I let Sean Wayne get away with murder when he was treating me really bad, but I let him have the house and everything so that he'd care for me. He didn't even bother coming home half the time, even though he knew I'd be stuck in my chair and in pain. When he was there, he was turning the house into some sort of second-hand car parts place, with oil and petrol over everything – a right mess – and clutter like you've never seen, making it really hard for me to move about and not fall over things.

The others would have a go at him about the dangerous state of the place and they'd tell him he needed to look after me properly, then he'd moan at me like mad about them. I wish he could have shown some kindness and not just used me for the carer's allowance and the cash I'd give him. When he knew he was in the wrong, he'd come crying to me, knowing that would soften me, and I'd tell him not to take no notice of the others.

And so, the cycle of abuse would keep going, around and around.

There it is – my life. First, my own dad, then the kids' dad, then the kids would start telling me what to do... I used to think, *Why me? All I've ever done is love them and care for them.* But I wouldn't have changed Ron or my kids, 'cos I really did love them all.

My only real regret is that I let Trevor go, but at least I found the opportunity to have a relationship with him later, and that's more than Ron was able to do with his fancy women's kids.

My kids have brought me heartache, but they've been good to me as well. Pat took me on my first holiday, Shaun and Wayne used to take me on day trips, Brenda and I would go shopping together, Nigel would cook Sunday lunch every week, and Dawn talked me into going to stay with her and Eric to recover from my illness and surgery – and they let me stay for the duration!

They cared for me, even took me to Disneyland, and Dawn taught me how to open my mouth if I wasn't happy with anything. To be honest, I've never shut it for a minute ever since because I knew I'd kept quiet for way too long before that.

It made me happy to see Nigel get off the drink after thirty years of being alcoholic, so I didn't have to lose another of my boys, like poor Georgie.

It cut me real deep when I got that awful letter from Diane, accusing me of killing our Georgie. Her words were torture but I couldn't ever destroy the letter. I just kept it.

One night Sean Wayne phoned Dawn's house to tell me that Nigel was blind drunk in Blakenhall, shouting his mouth off. What he didn't know was that Nigel had been with us all that week and hadn't touched a drop, so I told him he was a bastard liar, and I cut the call short, saying I needed to go to the toilet.

I had a bit of a cry, and I was really angry.

"Why do these lot have to keep causing trouble for each other? I'll tell you why! It's because they're all jealous of Nigel getting on with his life, and because he's not doing their dirty work for 'em no more."

Whenever Sean Wayne would pour out more of his lies, I'd blame that dirty whore, his missus, because he'd been much worse since he got with her. I hadn't realised that he'd been that way pretty much for years, because the others had made sure I didn't get to know about most of his antics.

It was great having Nigel to live with us, so I could keep an eye on him and keep him away from temptation, clear of "the blurr", as I called it – I said that was the noise they made when they were chucking up the drink down the toilet!

Seeing my boy off the drink meant he and I could have proper talks, and I was really pleased with his recovery and how he turned his life right around. He proved it is possible to break away from alcohol, from crime, homelessness, and from a violent relationship. He freed himself from all those who had held him back through their jealousy or whatever. I'd got my little lad back.

Just like Nigel accepted that he needed to change his life and recover, stay clean, so I accepted my own life with my illnesses and my limitations.

I saw Shaun and Wayne get really poorly, and those two were always so good at looking after other folk. Proper soft, the two of them, but I got to see them married, and Wayne's been like another son to me. I love them pair to bits.

Brenda was in a bad marriage but I saw her get out of that abusive relationship and she found a nice man who treats her right. So we got on better after that.

I've lost two of my kids – Georgie at the hands of a murderer and Ron to cancer, like his dad. Something you never want to have to do, is that... no mother should ever have to bury her kids.

It's been a lovely life for me, living with Dawn and Eric and the boys. Dawn's taught me a lot, like standing up for myself, feeling free to speak up, and we'd sit there, me and Dawn, discussing how each of us felt about the abuse we'd both suffered – now that's something I'd never been able to do before.

I reckon I'd always known that holding your tongue instead of talking about things and getting them out in the open was never a good idea, but when Dawn and I talked to each other about our feelings like that, I realised just how important it is to be honest with folk, and not to keep your thoughts to yourself, buried deep inside where they can turn bad.

My relationship with Dawn grew stronger, the more we talked and shared the things we'd both kept secret before. If people don't talk openly with each other, it causes idle gossip and wrong assumptions, then you get distance between folk, with doubts and questions left unanswered.

In my younger days, nobody would have been caught dead talking about sexual abuse. It was just something men did, and the women and girls had to put up with it, keep it as their dark secret or there would be hell to pay. When we first started to have our conversations, I felt really guilty about what Dawn had gone through because I blamed myself for letting it happen, for not doing something about it at the time. I'm pretty sure any mother worth her salt would feel the same.

I know now that if only people could be open and honest with each other over the things that matter, their relationships could be saved instead of falling apart, mental health problems could be dealt with earlier, and lives could be changed for the better – or even saved in many cases.

Most of all, after reading Dawn's book, I said I could write me a book that would make your hair curl! And Dawn's helped me to do just that as well.

I might not be here to read it, but I already know the story because I was the fool that lived it.

Doris Stanton, 2018

EPILOGUE

When Mom said those words, she must have sensed what was coming, because after she was diagnosed with terminal stomach cancer, the consultant told me and Nigel she would probably have four to six weeks to live. When she was told it was cancer, she said, "I'm not going anywhere yet, not until I'm ready." We never mentioned the actual timeframe to Mom.

Instead, I told her *It's just another ailment and we'll deal with it, just the same as your heart, your diabetes and your kidneys.* She seemed to be reassured when I reminded her that people live with cancer these days and they don't always die right away, because 'terminal' doesn't mean death, it means living with an illness that threatens your health.

Mom called herself *The Wisemore Girl* because she started her life in the Wisemore in Walsall. She always had many wise words, but one thing she told me that I'll always remember, is "Never forget where you come from."

She was wise with her words and she didn't forget her roots, never thought she was better than anyone else, except when she was fighting for her man! Then, she would have taken on the world.

She won friends like a human cyclone: whenever she crossed someone's path, she'd sweep them up with her charming, down-to-earth manner. Every child who met her was drawn to her like a magnet, she was "Nanna" to them all and she loved every one of them. I think she was kept going by reliving her own early childhood through them.

Down-to-earth, with no airs and graces, she called a spade a spade and she never beat around the bush if someone got on the wrong side of her. Whenever she upset them, some of the family would say she could start a fight in an empty house, because she didn't mince her words or hold back. And she only ever spoke the truth.

When things would get bad, she'd tell me, "What doesn't kill you makes you stronger" and "Ignore people's nasty comments – they're only jealous". She taught me to laugh at life.

Her advice, if someone was trying to annoy or rile one of us, was to ignore the insults and the taunts, and smile at them, "because that gets them mad and they'll go away a lot quicker!" Mom was like a smiling assassin!

In our many chats, Mom always said what a

beautiful life she'd had when she was a young girl, right up to when her mom died, and that's when it all went bad, when her dad started abusing her, so when I knew she was getting close to her time, I wanted her to be able to pass on with the same happiness around her as she'd known back then.

The night before she died, when she was ready, Mom asked me if I'd lie beside her in the bed, and she told me, "Dawn, I think this has got the better of me now, so I want to go." I did as she asked, but when I suggested we go to sleep, she said, "No, I want to go to Africa to look after them poorly babies." Always thinking of others, always wanting to help, that was Mom.

We lay there all night, listening to Al Jolson's *Tootsie,* because that was the song Dad used to sing to her, and I made her a promise, that all her children would be okay.

When the morning came, she woke up and asked where everyone was. "At school, at work – wherever they're supposed to be." She wanted to know if Brenda would be coming and I explained that Brenda had an appointment for a scan on that day. "What, on her fucking head, to see if there's a brain there?"

Her words weren't meant as nasty, she just wanted Brenda to stand up for herself and get rid of the idiots around her, the wasters hanging on to her. Mom saw herself in Brenda and she wanted her daughter to avoid following in her footsteps and ending up with a life like she'd had.

She fell asleep again and only woke once more, when Charlie's wife, Samantha, came into the room: Mom smiled at her, then went back to sleep.

Mom slipped away peacefully at 3.44 in the afternoon on the twenty-sixth of January, 2018, with me lying beside her. It was sad, but at the same time beautiful, to know she wasn't afraid any longer.

Just as she'd done for Dad with his funeral, we gave her a send-off to remember, with a horse-drawn carriage and lots of flowers, and so many people there to say goodbye to her. Just like she wanted. It really wasn't sadness for me, because Mom passed in such a lovely way, and she had her humour right to the end. I know she's at peace now with Dad, the man she adored, forgave and loved with all her heart.

When I was young, I was a daddy's girl and I didn't have a close relationship with Mom, but after Dad passed and she came to live with us, over the last ten years our relationship has grown from her being *parent* to *mom* then to *best friend*.

She encouraged me to publish my own book, *Breaking the Chain,* and she stood by me, and that's why I've helped her with this, her story, just as she told it to me, and I am publishing it as her legacy to everyone, as a tribute to a wonderful lady.

Sleep tight, Mom.

Dawn Parton, 2018

In Remembrance...

To my mom, my best friend
My guardian angel xxxx
Loved and missed so much
Love always,

Your daughter, Brenda

Yes, I'm your red-headed little git, the one who bought you your scratch cards – because I didn't want to be killed and buried in the garden, as you kept threatening me when I teased you! Remember that day when Dawn left my scratch card on your table while I was out, so you scratched it and won £50!! I came home with a card for both of us, mine won £10 and yours lost – you'd normally be in a mood about it but you just smirked and said you didn't care because you'd already won the £50 and put it away with your other winnings. I didn't mind, I would have given you the world if I could, because I loved you.

Thank you for not giving up on me when I was drinking, and for asking Eric if I could live with you all when I'd nearly killed myself with drink. I promised you I'd never touch another drop and I wouldn't tarnish your memory by going back on that.

When Dawn and I were told you'd got the cancer, it nearly killed me. You almost did see me off one night when you were poorly: I was eating a curry and suddenly you let out a really big sigh. It shocked me and my food went down the wrong way, making me choke. Dawn and Brenda checked on you and there you were, snoring away! They fell about in fits of giggles.

And that wasn't the last laugh you had at my expense, was it? The day you passed away I'd left my scratch card on the windowsill and, as you were taken out of the house, I noticed it was gone. I found it under your chair!

I've had three clean years now, those years I spent with you, my Mom, my hero. Love and miss you, but glad I had a mom like you. Goodnight, Tuts.

Nigel

Eric's thoughts...

You made our home a family home. I enjoyed our chats when you'd tell me about your childhood, growing up and the scrapes you got into. When we'd have the banter, you'd give me such beatings because I teased you and later, when I walked past you, I'd get a poke with your knitting needle to catch me unawares.

Your little smiling eyes when I pretended I'd left my scratch card on your table, while you scratched it and won, then hid it in your word-search book together with its "little brothers and sisters" as you called the winning cards. You saved them all up so you could go shopping for clothes, and when I was pushing you in your wheelchair you'd slam the brakes on by putting your feet down sharpish, nearly sending me flying over the handles. Anyway, you didn't need new clothes — your wardrobe was already bursting at the seams!

Thanks to your wise words, I got to reconnect with my own mother.
When our Harry was born, I remember saying to Dawn, "Look, with his smiling eyes he's like his Nanna Dutch." Ronnie gave you that name because you were treated like a duchess at ours.

Goodnight, God bless Ducharoo, until I see you again,

Love, Ecca the Drudge x

To Nana Doris,
We finally made it back to Blackpool for you. Even sitting on a windy pier, we remembered the times we had ice cream and you'd shout, "Gi's a lick!" and you'd smile.
You really have left something special in our lives, and Sam and I were honoured to spend time with you.
We hope you're watching over us in the years to come.
Love you to the moon and back, Nan
From your favourite grandkids,

Charlie and Sam

Nan, I love you and miss you loads.
I enjoyed spending time with you, playing prize bingo,
even if you did always win every game!
Hope you're back with Granddad now,
keeping him in line.
Goodnight, not Goodbye, with love from

Little Dawn xxxx

Nan, I'm sorry I didn't say goodbye,
but the pain was too much.
 I respected your wise words, even
when you were cussing me to get my
life together. I know you are reunited
with Granddad.
Fly high. Goodnight, our angel.
Love, Bobby *x*

Nan, you were so precious to us, even though we
didn't see you as much as we should have, and we
regret that a lot.
I remember how we used to come round and watch
you knit, and we'd try to help. We loved making you
cups of tea and getting things for you.
If we were naughty for our mum and dad, you
always made sure your walking stick was at hand –
ha-ha! then we'd run!
You were a brilliant nan, you always looked after us
when Mum and Dad asked you to, and we loved

coming round after school to play and sit on your lap watching TV, or playing with the fox you used to have.

I still have that nickname you gave me when I was a little kid – 'Monkey' LOL.

We love you, Nan, and we miss you but now you're with Granddad, happy again.

> *Love always,*
>
> *Granddaughter Teresa, Grandson Michael,*
>
> *Granddaughter Donna*
>
> *Xxxx*

Nanna Doris picked us up from primary school when we'd broken up for Christmas and we all went to Walsall – my brother, my sister, Mom, Auntie Dawn, Charlie and Harry, and Nanna Doris always got loads of turkeys. We had about 20 turkeys, and we carried them all through the town. My brother and Harry were in a pram, so Mom and Auntie Dawn took them out and put some of the turkeys in there instead. We were parked on the other side of town, and that seemed miles away back then...

We all ended up with 2 turkeys each, and the kids were running around, being naughty... it was really funny, good memories. I will always keep hold of every memory shared with Nanna Doris. She knitted my son a beautiful blanket and it's his favourite. Sadly, Doris never met him but I will make sure he knows who she was.

Nanna Doris was a very important person in my life, and will always remain just as important.

Becka xxxxx

I like to remember Doris (Nan) as she was in her chair, enjoying her shows, scratching cards and knitting. I would just sit there, listening to her talk, or maybe telling me what I should do! She would tell stories of Walsall — the kind you wouldn't normally hear — stories about the places, the people...

It's great to think of all those winning scratch cards!

Fly high, miss you.

Love, Wayne Marshall (Welsh Wayne)

One special memory I have from childhood is Dawn asking me back for tea when we were at Harden Junior school. Her mom made me feel so welcome then, and as the years rolled by, Doris always made me feel just as welcome and at ease in her home.

I will treasure those memories always.

Sleep tight, Cocka. Our paths will cross again one day.

Goodnight, God bless, Mrs Stanton xx

Diane

I would like to tell you about two special people in my life. To be honest, these two people saved my life, because at the time I was in a bad place.

Six and a half years ago, I met Dawn and Dotty. Dawn and I hit it off straight away and she became the big sister I'd always longed for. And what a special person Dotty was – when we met she was sizing me up to see if I was good or bad. Thank God, she knew I was good!

As days turned into months and months into years, I realised Dotty was the nan I'd always wanted; every time I saw her she put a smile on my face.

Dotty and Dawn made me part of their lives and part of their family, and to this day that means everything to me.

The stories Dotty used to tell me were so unreal, and the way she talked and laughed was simply amazing. My Nan Dotty might not be here now, but she will always be in my heart and my soul. I thank Dawn for allowing me to spend precious time making memories with them both. I love them both with all my heart and always will, because they never judged me.

There aren't too many special people in this world, and I am honoured to have met two of them.

Nanny Dot was a unique person and there will never be another like her.
Rest in peace, my Nanny Dotty, such a special person. Thank you for letting me spend so many happy years with you. Love you with all my heart and soul, and you will never ever be forgotten.

Clare xxxxxxxxx

She was a lady who will be remembered for many things that don't need to be said out loud to others. Her knowledge was vast and the people she loved had earned the time she gave them. An inspiration to all who met her, with her favourite saying,

"Don't ask unless you want to hear the truth, so flip the lot!"

I miss her now, and always will.
Thank you for being such a big part of my life and my children's lives. Thank you for being you.

Lisa xx

To a beautiful person with a heart of gold, who never had a nasty bone in her body.
Gone to a better place, no more pain but eternal peace and rest.
Sadly missed.

Paul

Thank you for always being there
for me, through the laughter and the
tears. Goodnight and God Bless,
                    MOM
Love always,

Colleen x

Whenever I saw you with Dawn, out and about in your
wheelchair, I'd say "Hello, how are you today?" and you'd
give me a thumbs up and say "I'm good, cock!" You were
always smiling, and I knew you were happy with Dawn
because I could see the love between the two of you.
I will always remember your shining smile, Doris.
Goodnight and God bless.

Pauline x

I used to love our chats and laughs at
the gate while she was knitting away
in her wheelchair. She really looked
after me when I moved to Greenock
Lane with my kids, and I love her
for that.

Carol

She was like an Enid Blyton novel — lots of stories.
She was a diamond with a wealth of knowledge,
but always down to earth and straight talking.

Maureen (Mo)

Goodnight, God bless, Petal.
Mom, love you forever and miss you.
Shaun & Wayne x

From the man of few words
to the lady of many. NAN X
Harry